IN QUEST OF REALITY

IN QUEST OF REALITY

BEING

THE WARRACK LECTURES ON PREACHING
DELIVERED IN THE THEOLOGICAL COLLEGES
OF THE UNITED FREE CHURCH OF SCOTLAND
SESSION 1923-24

BY THE REV.

JAMES REID, M.A.

ST. ANDREW'S PRESBYTERIAN CHURCH, EASTBOURNE
Author of *The Victory of God*, etc.

HODDER & STOUGHTON
LIMITED   LONDON

MADE AND PRINTED IN GREAT BRITAIN BY MORRISON AND GIBB LTD., EDINBURGH

PREFACE

THESE lectures were delivered in the United Free Church Colleges of Edinburgh, Glasgow, and Aberdeen, in the early months of 1924. My only excuse for giving them printed form, is the very kind response with which they met when they were delivered, and the requests that were then made that they might be published.

It is impossible to achieve freshness in a task which has produced such volumes as those of Dale and Phillips Brooks, to mention only two of a lecture series which has done so much to secure the spiritual and intellectual elevation of the preaching ministry.

I confess that I began to prepare myself for writing these lectures of mine, by taking down from my shelves all the works on preaching which I possess, but after dipping into them, I foresaw that to re-read them would make it impossible for me to make any progress. I therefore set them aside and determined to speak of the ministry as, from my own limited point of view and experience, it has appeared to myself. One only of the lectures is devoted to the technique of the art, as I cannot imagine that they should be confined to hints for preachers, and I have sought, in the limited space allowed, to deal with some wider aspects of the subject.

I have chosen the title which appears on this volume because it seemed to convey most clearly the object I had in mind, which was to discuss how a preacher may achieve reality in his work. The word " reality " may be in some danger in these days of being overworked, but the craving for it points to a cause which in part at least is responsible for the separation of pulpit from pew and for not a little of the drift from organized Christianity.

These lectures were written for students in preparation, but if the book should bring any help to any of my brethren in the ministry, I shall feel that my hesitation about publication has been wisely overruled.

I am greatly indebted to my friends, Rev. Professor Fearon Halliday, B.A., of Selly Oak Colleges, Birmingham, for his suggestions, and Mr. A. W. Yeo, of Hodcombe, Eastbourne, for reading the *MSS*. and proofs.

J. R.

CONTENTS

LECTURE I

THE PREACHER'S TASK

A COURSE of lectures on preaching may appear to beg two very important questions. The first is whether preaching is worth while —whether it still retains in these days the urgency and importance of a special vocation. The other question is, granted the value of preaching, is it the kind of art which can be taught or learned? There are people to-day who are sceptical on both these points, and doubts about them have stolen into the mind of many a preacher and are steadily undermining his confidence. The "foolishness of preaching" is a phrase that has never lost its sting, and it never had more point than it has for multitudes to-day. How much of that is due to the fact that preaching has in many cases lost touch with real life, it is difficult to tell. Few would deny that many people are preaching who have little or nothing to say—nothing, that is, which would spontaneously burn its way into utterance. We can be sure that the world simply will *not* take it for granted that preaching is a man's job, except as we convince them of the fact by the worth of our preaching ; and that will be worth little if we ourselves have lost the conviction that it is worth while or do not feel that its technique is so far within our capacity that we can face a working world with the self-respect of " a workman that needeth not to be ashamed." The day is fast approaching when no man will be able to hold up his head in the face of public opinion unless he knows he is making some worthy contribution to life.   Whether, in the eyes of a certain section, the preacher's work will ever be anything else than a sort of social parasitism is a question with which we need not concern ourselves here. The important thing is not what other people think about our work ; it is whether we ourselves are convinced that our vocation is a valid and worthy form of self-expression such as we can put our whole manhood into and such that, whatever its apparent success or want of success, we can lift up our hearts to God without reproach.

The first essential, then, of real preaching is the conviction that it is worth while. That is essentially a spiritual experience. It is born of our own experience of the gospel —our own vision of the truth, and nothing else will give it. " Necessity is laid upon me " : that is the final reason for preaching. We preach because we must. The truth compels us. We cannot go deeper into the matter than that. We cannot conduct a preaching ministry for a lifetime on less.

But there are certain ideas drifting about in the air to-day which tend to cut the nerve of a preacher's confidence in his own task. There is, for instance, the idea that the prevalence of books and newspapers which more or less deal with religion and the conduct of life make preaching unnecessary. Even if it were true that people can find enough light on the spiritual side of their nature from reading, the same argument would make all

political speaking, and all kinds of public
address, unnecessary. But we do not need
to look very deeply into the mind of the
average man to have the idea dissipated that
he knows anything either very much or
very deeply about God ; while the average
journalist who deals with religion is often
about twenty-five years behind the times
and spends half his energy belabouring
views which are almost extinct among
thoughtful religious people.

Another argument against the necessity of
preaching comes from the modern growth
of psycho-analysis. Preaching seems so impersonal, while the greatest need in the
healing of souls seems to be the need of
individual dealing. The pastoral office is
assuming, as it ought to do, much greater
importance, and some are asking whether
this is not the real work of the ministry.
One answer to this objection is that there
will be plenty of opportunity in any well-
ordered ministry for this kind of work. In
proportion as our preaching ministry is
effective, the need for spending time upon
individual cases will become more clamant.

But apart from this, there is no better or healthier self-analysis than that which a man makes for himself in the light of the revelation of Christ. The true preacher has a function as a healer of sick souls far more effectual and covering a wider range than he imagines. " God singles out unit by unit " even while we are preaching to a multitude, and there is no other way in which His truth can be so effectually set free to become the vehicle of the delicate personal dealing of the Spirit of God with men. It is a common experience for people to tell us that we seemed to be dealing with their very case, sometimes even accusing us of preaching at them, when as a matter of fact we were quite unconscious of their presence. There are instances which every preacher can give of cases where God has been manifestly at work in a way that has awed and humbled his spirit. Good preaching is extraordinarily individual and personal without our knowing it, for the effect of all true preaching is to bring people face to face with God, Who searches the hearts of men far more surely than even our best analytical skill can accomplish.

There is yet another idea which is sapping the confidence of some men in the ministry and, as we all know, is one which it is part of our business to teach—that all callings rank the same with God and that the age needs, above everything else, men who will carry the Spirit of Christ into the ordinary business of daily life. There are countless positions in business or professional life which present strategic points for advancing the Kingdom of God—positions which seem to offer the chance of a larger life and a wider opportunity than that of a minister, and we are tempted to wonder if we have not made a mistake. We see some who rubbed shoulders with us at college filling these positions ; we think of the poverty of result which often seems to attend our own ministry. We come to point after point in the ordinary course of preaching where we appear to have worked out one seam of truth and find ourselves faced with the need of driving a new mine with hardly a glimmer of ore, and we are tempted to lose heart. There are times when many a minister feels like writing his resignation. This temptation to doubt the validity of our call comes to all of us ; it is an inevitable result of the nature of the call to the ministry. We have to meet and over-come there the suggestion which besets all spiritual experience, that there is something in it of illusion. It is quite possible that this temptation may have been part of the desert experience of Christ, if the situation there were truly understood. We crave for signs that never come, and would not be of God if they did. This temptation can only be met by resources which are spiritual : it is an hour when we need to seek the recovery of our spirit in God. One thing is sure : the most fatal thing we can do is to doubt the validity of our call, or go back on a spiritual experience which sent us on the way. It is enough that we have put our hand to the plough. There were two ways, you remember, out of the Slough of Despond—which always lies somewhere or other on the road of a spiritual adventure. The one is backward to the place from which we have come. The other is forward, though it be but blindly ; but the forward way is the only way on which we can count on grasping the Hand of God.

Preaching is worth our while and all our while, however often we be beset by the whisper of doubt. Even if we were never meant to preach (supposing any man could say that with assurance—which is question-able) once we have started, the thing to do is to accept our situation : it is " to stop our ears against paralysing terrors and run the race that is set before us with a steady mind."   Above all, the way out of depression is to open our eyes afresh to the wonder of our message, which is the real root of the preacher's confidence and the only secret of his power. For what is preaching ? Phillips Brooks defines it as truth mediated through personality. It is the message of God com-municated by a person to persons, in public address. It takes two things to make it effective—the message and the man, and the one reacts on the other. The man shapes the message, but it will only be real preach-ing if at the same time the message is shaping the man.

I

What, then, is the preacher's task? That is our first inquiry. Our answer to it will be found in some clear view of our message. For our task is to proclaim a message; and to the message, both the method and the technique are subordinate; it is of little use thinking about these till we are clear about the message, for that will both make the preacher and shape his method.

Stevenson speaks of the struggle of truth " in a man " seeking expression: how it " tears and blinds him," rending its way into his books. The truth we have to speak will shape our utterance. It will determine a good deal of our method. It will, for instance, determine what kind of arguments shall or shall not be used. It will determine how a sermon shall be built up, what will be its emphasis, the direction of the appeal, the effect we are to aim at, the kind of response we seek to awaken. There is a kind of appeal which no preacher with a real message will ever use. There are methods which the truth will banish from the pulpit. There is a kind of success of which we will be ashamed. We cultivate, in time, a taste which censors and excludes vulgarities. On the other hand, there are appeals which might be banned by a severe and hypersensitive taste, which a preacher in earnest will employ without scruple.

In my college days, our deepest failure, if my own experience of the kind of atmosphere then prevalent among the students is any guide, lay along the line of a too rigid code of preaching conventions. A man who could hold an audience was suspected by his fellow-students of a defective intellectual outfit. The truth was not supposed either to tear or blind in the process of being born; it was often expected to freeze a man into a rigidity that passed for intellectualism. The favourite was the highbrow, who has been well defined as "a person who is educated beyond the limits of his natural intelligence."

The preacher's message is the revelation of God, and of God supremely in Jesus Christ, in all Christ was and did. We cannot better Paul's summary of his own message to the Corinthians—" Jesus Christ and Him

who is the crucified," to use Deissman's
translation.   That may sound a little narrow
and suggest the evangelism of the older school,
with its theories of the atonement from
which we have moved away.   We should not
be deterred on that account from facing the
fact that the heart of any real gospel is there.
It is not our business, of course, to preach a
theory, but a fact creating an experience;
and the creative redeeming fact is *there*.   It
is the character and activity of God towards
men, revealed in Jesus Christ, through His
life, death, and resurrection.   And the
central vision of God which Jesus came to
bring is that of the holy, personal Father.
Everything in real religion springs from that
—our view of the world, our valuation of
human personality, our way of duty, our
vision of immortality.   Our business is to
reveal God in Christ through our preaching,
in such a way as to bring men and women
into right relations with Him.

This seems the veriest commonplace ; but
even were it so, this central message remains
the most vital need of the pulpit to-day.   To
say that it is commonplace is no argument

against emphasizing it; as Dale said, it is
the great commonplaces by which we live.
Freshness and vitality in the pulpit are not
to be achieved by novel or *outré* themes, but
by the re-thinking and fresh presentation of
the oldest of themes. And one wonders
whether it is so commonplace as it appears.
The more deeply one looks into the mind of
this generation, the more one realizes that
people are wrong because they are out of
relation with God; and they are out of
relation with God because they have misunderstood the character of God and therefore the nature of right relations with Him.
All kinds of doubts and mistakes and perplexities can be traced to some wrong idea
of God. Most of the perplexities of a theological kind which were raised during the
war betrayed a mass of ignorance regarding
the Christian view of God : ignorance of those
who looked on Him as dominant impersonal
force and asked why He did not stop the
war ; and of those who looked on Him as
genial tolerant benevolence and wondered
why He ever allowed it to begin; as well as
of those who regarded it as a **judgment**

definitely sent to punish men for their neglect.
Many of our people are still worshipping a
half-pagan deity. The primitive in all of us
dies hard. There is a good deal of current
religion that is only baptized superstition and
it is found in all the churches. With many
people there is still an unresolved conflict
between the God of the Old Testament and
the God of the New. A host of questions
about prayer and suffering are vexing the
minds of people who would cease to ask
them if only they saw God in Christ. And
the only way to help them is to preach the
message of God in Christ. Once we have
seen Him there, we can see Him in His
dealings with the patriarchs, the kings, and
the prophets also. But we have no real
message, no authoritative vision of conduct
or life or duty, till we see them springing from
our true relationship to God. All religion
begins there. When Bradlaugh the atheist
was elected to the House of Commons, some
one moved that he be not allowed to take
his seat because he refused to take the oath
in the usual form, and remarked that " after
all, every one believed in a God of some sort

or another." Whereupon Gladstone took up
the cudgels for liberty, and rejoined that " to
believe in a God of some sort or another " is
no religion at all. Who is God ? What is
He like ? What is the " deep heart-shatter-
ing secret of His way with us " ? What kind
of activity is in the line of His real nature ?
How does He come to His glory ? What do
we mean by the Divine ? And—springing
from that—what is the true nature of man,
His child ? How should we bear ourselves
to one another if we be His children ? What
does sin mean, in the light of the revelation
of God in Jesus ? And how does He redeem
us from it ? How do we get back into
fellowship with Him, and how will that
fellowship be expressed in the daily round
and the common task, as well as in the
corporate relationships and activities of life ?
There is matter for our preaching here,
enough to take a lifetime to investigate
and all our highest powers to unfold and
proclaim.

I venture to lay stress on this as the
very marrow and substance of our preaching,
not once in a while, but all the time—the

proclamation of God the Father and His relations with His children. The times in which we live demand it as never before. No one can look at the religious world to-day without seeing that we are coming to a parting of the ways. The question at issue is whether we are going to recover for our age all that is involved in a sane and healthy Protestantism — despite some unfortunate associations of the name—or whether we are going back to what is really a religion of magical operation and external authority. The main point at issue in the controversy about Church union lies there. The root of religious uncertainty lies there. It is really a question of the nature of God and His relation to men and to His world. Does He govern them from without and save men by a succour which is independent of the response of their own personality and does not require the apprehension of truth through their own insight? Or, on the other hand, does He rule men through love in a free obedience as His children, and save them—by no magical grace and no external force applied through fear or authority—but only through a love that bears their sin and has no other power to win them but the persuasions presented in the Cross ? That is really the question of our time which underlies everything. People are drifting out of the true Protestant position because Protestantism demands insight, and a clear and reasonable grasp of the truth in this vision of a personal suffering love. We simply cannot hold people to a reasonable religion unless we set them thinking with their own minds.

Perhaps the gravest charge which can be laid against what we may call the Protestant section of the Church during the last quarter of a century, is that it has not taught the people to think. It is often said that the sermon occupies too important a place in the service, and that too little emphasis is laid on the devotional side of worship : and this has sometimes been made an excuse for people drifting into communions where ceremonial occupies a large place, to say nothing of their substitution of an external authority for individual insight in the guidance of life. The real remedy for this defect in our service does not lie in a poorer quality of preaching. On the contrary, it is often the quality of the preaching which has produced the true dissatisfaction. Listening to a really good sermon may be a very real devotional exercise. The preaching of the last generation has too often been nebulous, scornful of systematic doctrine, aiming only, as a rule, at producing a certain inspirational result by an emotional uplift, and providing a kind of tonic for a depressed or jaded spirit. A speaker not long ago at a great religious assembly said that he had been listening to sermons all his life and the only impression they had left on him was a kind of " grey patch on his brain " ! We have become the slaves of what is called " practical preaching," almost to the extent of banishing clear and consistent thought. We have been afraid to make people think. The result is that preaching has ceased to supply what people need if they are to grow strong in the freedom of the children of God, as well as grounded and settled in a faith which is their own. The clamant need of our time is for more central preaching — preaching which will educate insight and quicken the springs of character in the varied response of children to the Father. A traveller tells us of a curious mirror of silver he picked up in Japan ; this, when flashing the light, reflected, not a mere beam, but the image of the god Buddha that had been subtly wrought into its texture. Good preaching should have the supreme quality of reflecting the vision of God the Father.

It is only through this vision of God that we have any key to those perplexities of Christian duty which are met in every sphere of life. A score of problems of Christian conduct await solution. To take only one or two—the attitude of men to the industrial problem, to the international problem, to the problems of crime and war, will all depend on the view they take of God and His method and purpose. All life is capable of being interpreted on this basis of God's Fatherhood revealed in Jesus. Only so seen, can life become intelligible. Only so can we bring to bear on human strife and unbrotherliness the light by which the world can find its way to peace and real progress. Only so can we give to men and women the clue to the thing they most of all need, which is to know the meaning of their own life. It is our business to show them that this message of God's nature, and the consequent nature of man, with all that it demands of love and brotherhood, is no airy dream, but the unveiling of basic reality and consequently the only foundation on which we can safely build anything that will stand. For some people such a message will literally be a new revelation. It will come to them with wonder and surprise. Mr. Dan Crawford in one of his books tells of the thrill it gave him to preach the gospel to people who had never heard anything like it before. We will experience the same kind of thrill to-day. For to many people—people inside our churches as well as outside of them—this whole view of God's loving personal relation to us, and all it involves, will come as good news, with all the glad surprise of light in a cloudy day. To others again whose theology has been of the older school, it may mean a gradual reconstruction of their whole outlook on God and on life—a thing not to be

attained without some pain and difficulty.
But whatever the immediate reaction of our
preaching, we must present this message of
God to men in such a way that they shall
find all their self-made shelters broken down
and their inhibitions taken away. There
is a love of God in every man, sometimes
repressed, but always present in experience though often unrecognized, which is
waiting to rise up and call God Father in
deed and in reality. When people, like the
prodigal, come to themselves, they rise and
go to the Father, and when they go to the
Father, they come to themselves. We can do
nothing for men except in the measure in
which we relate them to Him.

In this task we will, of course, direct our
message first of all, and all the time, to the
conversion of the individual, for it is an
incontrovertible fact that the world in the
long run can only be changed by changing
individuals. We must aim at bringing
each single one into a right relation with
God. Our first objective—indeed our main
objective—is to seek men and women one
by one as Jesus sought them and so to

find them that they shall seek others. A ministry which is not a converting ministry, turning men and women individually to God, has failed in its most vital task. But we have other work to do also. It is to reach the mind of a group—large or small—and leaven it. From the pulpit we may have an opportunity of getting into touch with the thinking mind of a community. We may leaven them by the truth, raising the whole standard of their life, teaching new values. Our influence may soak in almost unconsciously—till men find themselves reading their newspapers with a different outlook—sometimes, it may be, changing their newspapers ! We may find them taking a new stand in a municipal election, beginning to think in terms of people instead of rates, taking a new line about international problems, thinking differently about war, growing a conscience about stocks and shares, and asking questions about how their money is made and what they are doing with it when it is made. These results are definite and direct fruits of the gospel. We reach people from many different sides,

There are no stereotyped gates into the kingdom.

> " For not through eastern windows only
>   When daylight comes, comes in the light ;
> In front, the sun climbs slow, how slowly,
>   But westward, look, the land is bright."

Both results are to be aimed at in preaching—the definite personal relationship to God in Jesus and the changing of the mind and outlook of people till they begin to think with the mind of Christ. Sometimes the truth first comes home in the sense of a new personal relation to God which gradually grows till everything in the man's world is changed. Sometimes his world is changed bit by bit through a new outlook, and then one day he finds God in it : but the work is not completely done till both things happen, and men and Christ go hand in hand through a world which is altogether new.

For that task of relating men to God, the message of God in Christ is our only instrument, and it is all we need. We can have no other authority in preaching than the truth. We can have no other appeal by which to win men for the kingdom than the truth ; no other confidence as we face an audience than the confidence born of the truth.

In general cases the first thing we have to do is to get people to *see* the truth—really to see by the eyes of spiritual perception the love of God in Christ. That means, for many, a rebirth—a conversion—a real awakening. We are confronted to-day with a mass of spiritual needs of different kinds; the troubles of the soul are many and varied. But in one form or another the real trouble is blindness. The spiritual perception is not quickened. We come to realize in our ministry, before long, that people either see or they do not see. Sometimes they only see dimly, but they see. But, again and again, we have to face the fact that they do not see at all. Their trouble, as Paul found in the case of the Corinthians, is that the message is to them either a " scandal " or a " piece of folly." They may apprehend it with the intelligence, but only as a system of thought. It is not a living fact. They do not know God. Religion simply does not count at all. The message of the love of God in Christ crucified is just " sloppy folly," as a certain distinguished man put it the other day. That is, quite frankly, how some people look at the message of Jesus. They cannot see the truth : they are the heartbreak and the perplexity of our ministry, and we find them sometimes drifting out of our churches, after years of teaching and apparent acquiescence, because they have not seen God in Jesus. How are we to get hold of them ? How are we to make them see ? Only by the truth and the whole truth expressed in the phrase, " Christ and Him crucified." The truth has the power to awaken its own sense of need ; we can depend on it. It is our business so to reveal it as to help them to see. Some one said the other day that a rediscovery of what Christ meant by faith would bring a revival of religion. There is something in that. But there is a prior work to be done. Faith is only our natural response to the vision of God in Jesus. That vision alone will awaken faith as a natural result. Can any one really see Christ without having the impulse awakened to trust Him ? And there is a moral regenerating power in the message of

the truth in Jesus, in the reality of His love
for men as seen in Calvary—where alone it
reaches its point of flame against the background of human sin—which can melt the
very hardest heart.   There lies our power.
We are all familiar with the argument for
what is called the social gospel.   There are
people so enmeshed in an evil environment
that they need almost to be dug out before they
can begin to see the light and to be cared for,
like a suffocated man, till they are at the
point where their souls can function normally
enough to breathe the spiritual atmosphere
for themselves.   But social service can never
take the place of the message of the gospel
of God's love.   Social service only reaches
real effectiveness as it becomes, so to speak,
the hands and feet of the messengers of God—
a medium through which the love of God is
made real, conveying the touch of Jesus.
As such it is an essential element in the
revelation of God the Father.   But, however
far down they be sunk, never for a moment
let us give people up as beyond the reach of
the truth of God *just where they are*.   There
is a penetrative power in that light which

can reach the deepest dungeon. A wonderful illustration of this fact came to light lately in a little book called *A Gentleman in Prison*. A desperate criminal in a Japanese prison, condemned to death for murder, was visited by two lady missionaries. They spoke to him, but found him cold and indifferent. They left with him as they went a copy of the New Testament. One day, in boredom mixed with curiosity, he took down the New Testament and opened it, and the story of what happened is told in one of a series of letters which he left behind. He began by reading the Parable of the Lost Sheep. " Still," he says, " I was not sufficiently impressed to have any special belief in what I was reading. I simply thought they were words which any preacher might have used. I put the New Testament on the shelf again and did not read it for some time. A little later, when I was tired of doing nothing, I took down the book again and began to read. This time I read how Jesus was handed over to Pilate, was tried unjustly, and put to death by crucifixion. As I read this, I began to think. This person they called Jesus was evidently a man who at any rate tried to lead others into the paths of virtue, and it seemed an inhuman thing to crucify Him, simply because He had different religious opinions from others. Even I, hardened criminal that I was, thought it a shame that His enemies should have treated Him in this way.

" I went on, and my attention was next taken by these words : ' And Jesus said, " Father, forgive them, for they know not what they do." ' I stopped. I was stabbed to the heart as if pierced by a five-inch nail. What did the verse reveal to me ? Shall I call it the love of the heart of Christ ? Shall I call it His compassion ? I do not know what to call it. I only know that, with an unspeakably grateful heart, I believed. Through this simple sentence I was led into the whole of Christianity. This is how I thought it out. I suppose a man's greatest enemy is the one who seeks to take his life from him. There is surely no greater enemy than this. Now at the very moment when Jesus' life was being taken from Him, He prayed for His enemies to the God of heaven, ' Father, forgive them, for they know not

what they do.' What else could I believe
but that He was indeed the Son of God ? "

Never mind his rationalizing, if you call it
so. The thing that happened was, that he
saw God in Jesus the crucified, and seeing
Him was changed into another man. There
is the miracle, for the production of which
our preaching is to be the vehicle. And the
power that can do it, even in a dungeon and
in a criminal's heart, is the power of the
truth breaking in to open the blind eyes.
It is worth a lifetime's study and a life laid
down, to become the instrument of such
reconciling love, and no art that produces
any other impression, though it bring us to
heights of popularity, can compare with the
preaching of a man who brings even one
soul into right relations with God. But my
point is that the truth is its own searchlight ;
the truth alone, without compromise—without regard to popular demand. The real
question about a man's message is not
whether it is what the people want, nor even
whether it is edifying, but whether it is true.
Our business is with nothing less and with
nothing more, though of course to see it

and present it in all its range and power will take all the sinews of our mind and soul.

II

Now with this for a central aim, there are certain general rules which I venture to set down.

1. Our preaching must be *clear and simple*. If the truth is to have its appeal, the people must see it in the clearest way. Nothing is going to reach the conscience which is not pellucidly clear to the mind. Some one says that " what is spiritually necessary may be intellectually unintelligible." That is at least a very dangerous principle. There is a distinct peril lest, having banished magic from our cultus, we should enshrine something very like it in our vocabulary. " These be good words," says an old woman in *Silas Marner*. We are tempted to use certain phrases and terms familiar to ourselves, which to the people are either unintelligible, or else so crusted, like a ship with barnacles, with hoary superstition or pious association of a distinctly unattractive kind, that they carry people nowhere. To-day we are

in the new psychology. She had read five or six books, but she was held up on every other page by the fact that she did not know the language terms, and she wanted to know if there was a simple book which would explain them. That is precisely our difficulty in preaching. The Bible itself is largely a closed book to some people for the same reasons ; the Epistles of St. Paul are a striking example. There is hardly a phrase of Biblical theology which we can take for granted. Take such terms as " sin," for instance, or " grace," or " coming to Christ," or " the Kingdom of God," or " eternal life," or " conversion," or " faith." What do they mean ? This is fundamental work ; but we will find an astonishing response of interest in tackling such phrases and giving new meanings to old terms. We can preach a whole series of sermons, answering questions which have thus become elementary. And every one of them will be for some people in our congregations a window into a new country. It will throw floods of light on sealed pages. It will unwrap graveclothes to give dead words life. Think of the preaching of the first apostles described in the Acts. What was the secret of its power? The people acknowledged that they heard the apostles "talking, each man in his own tongue, of the triumphs of God." Real preaching is talking to people in their own language of the triumphs of God. Words must stand for real things if preaching is to be real. They must not merely be the symbols of what, to many people, is either a theological figment or an unintelligible mystery. Whatever the gift of tongues was, clear speech is part of the means by which the message of God breaks through everything and wins its way past " clay-shuttered doors."

2. A second rule that should be followed is that real preaching must be *positive*. The truth must be trusted to do its own work of correcting error or of self-defence. Two types of sermon commonly err on the negative side. The one is the argumentative sermon which aims at establishing a case by stating objections and meeting them. This type of preaching requires the greatest of care. The danger is that stating objections for the

3

purpose of meeting them may only result in sowing our own doubts ; for the capacity of the average hearer to follow an argument is limited. There is a place, of course, for the apologetic sermon, but it must not be forgotten that the sphere of apologetics is limited. Its true function is to prepare for the evangel, to remove obstacles out of the way of the man who is seeking the light. It is really only valid and worth while for those who " ask the way to Zion with their faces thitherward." That is the point. People must be sincere ; they must be seeking truth, before our arguments will help to remove their objections. An apologetic sermon is of very little use to a man to whom doubt is not an agony, and that man is already on the way to the truth. For people who want to find the truth, who want to believe, but to whom the way is blocked by intellectual difficulties, the right kind of argument can be an enormous help. It can bring a unity into their world, which is generally what is needed by those who have doubts. Some people stand on the threshold of the Kingdom, and it only needs the build-

ing of some bridge, or the demolishing of
some barrier, to bring them into it. They
are there already in spirit, but they have
intellectually what the Quakers call " a stop
in their mind." A well-known scientist of
our day confesses, in a little book, that for
years he had been unable to accept
Christianity till he found a bridge, as he
puts it, over the Rubicon into the Christian
faith. His particular bridge was an argument for the truth of the Incarnation. It
is a bridge which he confesses many others
might smile at; he is disappointed, in fact,
because it does not seem to appeal to certain
learned theologians to whom he has explained it. But it served his purpose, which
was to put down a plank on which his feet
could cross into the country where his heart
was really dwelling. Once over, he no longer
needs it. There is a place in such cases for
the right kind of apologetic. Or, again,
there are people who are uneasy lest their
faith or their experience should be a kind of
illusion. They want to have the foundations
examined to see that the structure has its
base in a reasonable world. Or, yet again,

there are people who stand outside because
they have never thought very deeply about
religion. They have been put off by some
catchword or some stupid objection which is
really a blind, though they do not know it.
And by argument or attack it is possible to
demolish that barrier and make them think
of God. We can help a great many people
just by making them think.

But, when all is said and done, argumentative preaching can never bring a man
into the spiritual world : it cannot be the
basis of faith. In the long run the truth
is the only apologetic for the purposes of
preaching. All the stock arguments against
Christianity begin to vanish into thin air
when a man has seen Jesus. Argument may
demolish the barriers that hide ; it can
prepare the way of the Lord ; it can never
reveal Him ; nor in the last resort prevent
the man who is on the defensive against the
truth from erecting other barriers. For
there are people for whom, like the woman
of Samaria, religious difficulties and dis-
cussions are a refuge from a moral challenge.
In a letter to one of his preachers, John

Wesley quotes a bit of advice his father gave him when he was young : " You think to carry everything by dint of argument. But you will find, by and by, how very little is ever done in the world by clear reason." And Wesley adds : " Very true indeed." Positive truth alone, shining by its own light, quickening the perceptions, enlightening the eyes, is the argument which has the power in the long run. There is a very definite danger that the preacher who pays too much attention to the person with religious difficulties and gives himself to the building up of logical bases for truth, may be keeping people from resting on the true foundation, which is an experience and not a syllogism.

A word must be said of sermons of another negative type—sermons which are denunciatory or pugnacious. The psychologist has a startling commentary on stridency in the pulpit ; he puts it down to a conflict in the preacher himself, or, at least, to a subtle want of confidence in the truth. Be that as it may, sarcasm, or irony, or vehement condemnation, is a mistake. A text which gives a chance for invective is very attractive, especially when we are young. It may be questioned whether it ever does any real good. People generally apply it with unction to their neighbours and applaud the preacher's courage. Those who in sincerity take the message to themselves will probably not deserve it; or, if they do, may only be embittered or discouraged. To quote Wesley again : " I have often repented of judging too severely but very seldom of being too merciful." It is true that Jesus could denounce, but He did it, as we know when we get behind the scenes, with a breaking heart. No one would plead for soft words and honeyed accents. The truth will hurt ; it will probably wound. There is no preaching worth doing to-day which will not have for its first effect a quickening of conscience among religious people, bringing them face to face with a moral issue in things which many have been accustomed to look upon as neutral ground. But denunciation will never do it. It is the same with the wrong views which people hold : you can only meet and overcome them by the truth — the truth which is already rooted in the false view and which is really giving to the latter its power. Denounce the grotesque ideas associated with Christian Science as we may, the question a man who is drawn that way will ask us, is what we have to put in its place. Many of our most flagrant errors are only the refuge for a mind that has been deprived of the fulness of the truth.

In the biography of Dr. John Clifford, lately published, there is a quotation from his diary describing some sermons to which he had listened. In particular he tells of hearing " a sermon on Acts iv. 12 : Salvation through Jesus and salvation only through Jesus. The sermon was an attempt to expose the hollowness and uselessness of expedients for salvation, *e.g.* (1) Governmental changes ; (2) improvement in external circumstances of men ; (3) education ; (4) metaphysical culture ; (5) refinement. There was much of everything except Christ. All these other forces were treated as though they could do no good to any one. It was a most unsatisfactory sermon, calculated to alienate all young and reflective minds. It lacked balance ; worst of all, it lacked Christ. And yet I do not doubt the preacher felt that he was preaching the gospel. . . . The more I think of last night's sermon the more I see the urgent need for reform in preaching." Much could be said of such a line of argument as that suggested above, from the point of view of its truth. For who in these days would deny the influence of the Spirit in any one of these things which were condemned? Yet that is not what I am concerned with at the moment. The point I would make is, that to take up a large part of a sermon with a discussion of what the gospel is *not* is an entirely barren method, depressing and unenlightening. If the treatment of a subject seems to demand that misrepresentations or false ideas be first cleared out of the way, this should be done as briefly as possible and merely to make a pathway for the positive message. The presentation of Jesus and His message can safely be trusted to dethrone the false idols.

> " For oh ! the Master is so fair,
>   His smile so sweet to banished men,
> That they who meet Him unaware
>   Can never turn to earth again."

The cardinal fact about the gospel is that it is a gift. God comes to men seeking them. He has taken the initiative. Religion is not primarily a problem to be solved : it is a gift to be received. There is a way of preaching which leaves the impression that the truth is something so mysterious that only those who are willing to face an intellectual struggle, not far short of the heroic, can fathom the secret ; whereas it is something that will unfailingly meet men's needs in such a way as to convince them of its authority, if only they will be sincere with it. We carry to men in the Name of the Lord a message that makes them conscious of infinite Divine resources. That is what makes it a gospel. The demand God makes springs out of the gift God offers. His love creates the sense of duty, and provides the power that makes duty the joyful exercise of our souls in freedom. That message that we must work out our own salvation can be preached only in the light of the primal fact that God is working in us. God is a Redeemer Who is out to find us, if only we will allow ourselves to be found ; in Him also is the grace to

conquer the last citadel of our unwillingness ;
so that all we want to meet the deepest need
of our intractable wills and spiritually de-
pleted natures, is in Him. The all-sufficiency
of God to find men wherever they are and
bring them to Himself, is the very core of
the gospel.

3. This brings me to say that real preaching must be *thorough* ; it must go to the
root of the situation and must meet it with
the whole counsel of God. We can only help
people by the full message of God in Christ.
The temptation that besets us is to dwell on
some aspects of the truth to the exclusion of
others, till the truth becomes distorted. We
may dwell, for instance, on the Fatherhood
of God in such a way that God becomes
only a genial kind of parent who will tolerate
almost anything in his child, and whose very
forgiveness is only what Stevenson describes
in the old laird of Ballantrae as " the tears
of senility." Perhaps there is no word that
needs more emphasis in our day than the
exhortation : " If ye call on God as Father,
pass the time of your sojourning here in

fear." On the other hand, it is possible to state the necessity for repentance in such a way as to make people think that God is merely concerned with wounded feelings. Men are not going to be won into the Kingdom of God by abstracting this or that truth from the message. The gospel can do very little for people who will not allow it to do everything. People cannot be saved to-day from the things from which many of them are crying to be delivered, except by a full entrance into the real secret of Christianity. Only the fulness of the Christian message can really help people. Let me give an illustration or two of what I mean. We take it for granted that the gospel ought to deliver men from fear ; and so we preach it. " Be not afraid," we say to people who are shrinking from some threatening terror in a world of risks. We preach to them the care and love of God. But to tell them that and nothing more will do little for them except build a kind of shelter behind which they tremble still and which the first big trouble will blow down. Faith in God thus preached is a very leaky ship in which to put to sea on a very dangerous ocean. And there are a great many people to whom faith is just that—an unreality by which they preserve with difficulty an unstable equilibrium they call peace. We have to go further. What is this love of God, and what is God in His love seeking to do for us? His is obviously not a love that merely seeks to keep us safe and comfortable, but a love that is out for our character as His children. And there is no peace till we see that and consent to it; which means, of course, a new valuation of life, and a new conception of the love of God—in other words, the acceptance of the outlook of Jesus both on God's love and on life's ideal. Outside of that, to speak of God's care of us is mere sentiment which only keeps the trouble quiet, but does nothing to cast it out.

Or take the message of forgiveness. To many people it is an unreality because they are still conscious of the external results of sin, and it is from these that they are really seeking to be delivered. Or, in other cases, it is a mere shelter from punishment in the future life which they are seeking.

But there is no power in forgiveness till it means restoration to the fellowship of God through a new attitude that is ready to face the sin with all its consequences, and is at peace because there is nothing more to hide. This means, however, seeing the good of life in fellowship with God and in the way of righteousness, whatever it may cost ; it means insight into the real meaning of sin as estrangement from Him.   No cheap and easy gospel, no genial proclamation of pardon, will produce the peace which is the peace that passeth understanding, and not a sham or a hypocrisy.

Christianity is going to mean nothing as power in the world except as it saves men into the mind and attitude of Jesus through and through, and this involves a change which nothing but the full message of God's grace can produce and nothing but the fulness of His love can sustain. Christianity cannot survive at all in a world like this, upon an emasculated gospel or a message which is reduced to a few genial observations about the love of God. The question for us is whether we are going to trim our preaching to enable men and women to carry on with a certain amount of cheerfulness and courage and hope, calling them to " the task of happiness," or some such thing ; or whether we are going to ask them to face life in right relations with God the Father revealed in Christ crucified. With all due respect and admiration for these writers, we cannot get a gospel for the redemption of the world out of Stevenson's philosophy or Kipling's challenge to be a man. The message of God to men cannot be prostituted into " a handy book for the successful merchant," nor into the inspiration to help a nation to win a war, nor into a panacea for life's ills, nor into a means for supplying a world with comfortable amenities, nor indeed into any kind of re-inforcement to the spirit of man on the high road of his own ambition or his own self-chosen way of life. The Christian life is " eternal life in the midst of time, by the strength and under the eyes of God."

It is our difficult task to call people out to do business in great waters. Only as they are willing to follow, can we help them

to see " the works of the Lord and His
wonders in the deep." It is no easy am-
bassadorship. In the Covenanting times,
you remember, a certain travelling merchant
reported on preachers he had heard. Each
had his own peculiar quality. " One showed
me the majesty of God, another the loveli-
ness of Christ, and another showed me all
my heart." You will need to combine all
three before you will get a gospel for this
age or any age. This age of ours, however,
has this peculiar advantage as a field of
operations, that it is heartsick of unrealities
and is not nearly so afraid of being hurt.
For many of the old shelters have been
blasted down, and countless people are out
in the open, seeking, not for a covert from
the stormy blast, but for a heart of peace in
the midst of strife—a life which is storm-
beaten and yet secure. Nevertheless, you
will be tempted to the easy way of popularity
and quick returns which has made ship-
wreck of many a promising ministry. You
will be tempted (as the Roman Church in her
mission was tempted and fell) to a way of
preaching which aims at making people

comfortable in their souls rather than right with God, at taming the beast in man instead of transforming him, at helping people to walk by safe rules of good conduct instead of in the adventurous freedom of the Spirit. To take the other way may mean for the time being smaller congregations, and a Church which is only a spiritual remnant, though signs are not even now wanting that there is a revival waiting the true message.   But whatever it means, our aim in the ministry of preaching is nothing less than this, " that they being rooted and grounded in love may be able to comprehend with all saints what is the height and breadth and length and depth, and to know the love of Christ which passeth knowledge, that they may be filled with all the fulness of God."

LECTURE II

THE PREACHER'S AUDIENCE

IT is a mere commonplace to say that if we are to preach to men and women we must know them. If we are to be " fishers of men," which was Christ's own phrase for His apostles, we must know the nature and habits of the fish. The primary need of an effective sermon is that people must listen to it. We must get their attention. And we can only get their attention by appealing to their interests. In plain words, a sermon must be interesting. It is useless to excuse ourselves for being dull by saying that people are not interested in a religious subject. Even if that were true, which it is not, we have got to make them interested. That is what preaching is for. I appreciate fully the suggestion that a congregation can do very much to help us in advance by a willing attention—by a strenuous effort to overcome

4

those persistent voices from the outer world
that prevent the quiet recollection and concentration upon God. " Happy is the man,"
says George Eliot, " who has an audience
that demands his best." There are congregations all over the country which, if only
they would bring with them a spirit of ex-
pectant attention, could change the whole
atmosphere of their churches ; they would
turn many a dispirited messenger of Christ
into a flaming prophet. All that is true.
But that does not absolve us from the task
of securing their interest. We have the
people there without going out to seek them.
They would not be there in days like these
if there were not at least the suggestion of
a hunger hid away somewhere behind the
abstracted look. But we have no right to
presume upon their attention. If we were
going to the streets with our message, we
should not *primâ facie* look for attention.
We should set about creating it or should
expect to lose the audience. And we have
no right to count on people listening to a
sermon just because we have prepared it, or
because *we* happen to be interested in it ;

nor dare we presume upon the zeal or good-nature of a congregation so far as to give them ill-digested abstractions or imagine they will receive a message in any form in which we happen to offer it. In point of fact they will not, and by a psychological law they cannot. If they do not set about finding an interest, we must create it for them. Many sermons fail just here, because the people are not interested in the subject, and the reason why they are not interested in the subject is often, if the truth were told, because the preacher is not interested in *them*. A very true description of the difference between an effective minister and an ineffective one is that the former is more interested in people than in ideas, while the latter is more interested in ideas than in people.

We have got to find interests, then, in the minds of the people before us. We have got to find them also in real things—things that matter. And the interest must be a religious interest. It is no use knocking at doors to get a hearing for God, where He cannot well enter in. We can get people interested on the wrong side of their nature by stirring up feelings and enthusiasms it is useless to awaken. We must be on the alert to find a spot where a man's nature is " alive unto God." It may be some sore point, or some spiritually sensitive point, or, on the other hand, some point of aspiration where their nature is just waiting to break into a flame of faith.

For let us remember the Gospel is good news to be received with welcome, and it is good news because it speaks to a condition of human need. " As living water to a thirsty soul "—that is the kind of metaphor which describes it. It is not something to be argued about or received with blind credulity; it is truth which meets some ultimate need of the human soul and proclaims its authority in its power to satisfy it. We cannot, there-fore, preach to men's condition unless we can diagnose their need and so proclaim our gospel as both to unveil it and supply it.

For that purpose we must *know* men and women. How we are to win that knowledge is part of the making of a preacher, with which I will deal later. Some of us have had experience of life from other points of view than that of college training. That is invaluable. We should take every opportunity we can of learning about business, about other professions than our own, of the way in which people live, how they look at things, what they are thinking, where the yoke of life galls the raw flesh. A preacher will make little of it who has not taken the trouble to know, as intimately as he can, the peculiar problems and difficulties which his people meet with in their daily callings. He will put his foot in it very badly and make many a false appeal. Half his time he will be talking in the air. Nothing can be worse than to attempt to deal with a situation we do not know. Confidence will be shattered at a blow, and an air of unreality created which will perpetuate the fatal habit of looking at a sermon from a detached point of view as if it were spoken in a vacuum, and were not intended to be taken seriously. There is the other danger, of course, which is to confine ourselves to tame abstractions which may sound very sublime, but never reach any tender or sensitive spot, or convince a hearer

Him just where they are, within the frontiers
of their own world as they live in it day by
day. We must take it for granted that we
are speaking to people who have God in
their lives, at the moment, in some recog-
nizable element of experience. We can be
sure of this, there is a vital point where
God is meeting every man at the moment,
in something which he perhaps has not
recognized for the Divine, and we have
got to lay hold of that, somehow, and
illumine it :

"Till God breaks through it and makes it store
   To the heart that was starving in darkness before."

To make God a living reality is our business,
and we can only achieve it in the measure
in which we are able to reveal His Spirit,
even now, pulsing through the stuff of life.
Modern psychology has laid open an enormous
field in this respect, though it, like every
newborn science in the omniscience of its
youth, is in some quarters attempting to
step beyond its sphere and to make affirma-
tions about religion which it has no business
to make, because that is not its province.
We shall have to meet the suggestion that

all man's experience is explained by the un-conscious without reference to God, which is no more the case than that a spring in the hillside is explicable without the rain that comes from the heavens. The psychologist has no more right as psychologist to declare that his science explains the origin of experience, than the evolutionist had in Darwin's day the right to declare that his theories explained the primal origin of the world. The true function of psychology is really one of helping people to make the right adjustment to life so that reality can make its own appeal to them. Its business is to help men into an attitude of sincerity in relation to the world through which God reveals Himself. There is no doubt of a man's response to the Christian message which is presented to him if only he will be sincere with it. That was the reason why the one thing that Jesus asked of people was that they should be sincere—open to the light from whatever quarter it might come, and whatever demands it might bring ; that response of sincerity with the truth being the one response which it is within the power of every man to make.

I

Nothing, however, can keep us right and preserve our perspective, or give us such intimate knowledge of men, revealing us to them, and them to themselves, as the study of Jesus in His world of men. Men are, what they are in the presence of Jesus ; and the Gospels in their sincerity have preserved in the presence of Jesus His revelation of the thoughts and intents of the heart. In the Gospels with Him we are in a real world where human nature stands out in a light which makes that world a mirror of humanity for all time. We shall see there the things that shaped His message and perpetuated it. In a real sense, every word He spoke, and everything He did, was related to some need or trouble or defect in the lives of men around Him, calling forth the revelation of the heart of God which could deal with it. And the gospel stories were primarily recorded and kept alive because of the existence of these same needs and defects in the world of the early Church which wrote these stories down.

What, then, are the elements which He

found in human life and which are still, to-day, the objective of our message and the living points of our appeal ?

First of all, perhaps, there is *fear* ; and, allied to it, the fungus growth of care ; both of which have their being in a world which is empty of the sunlight of a clear vision of God. How much these were in Christ's mind as an objective of His message, you can trace in the number of times He dealt with them. Again and again He attacked both fear and care. Some of the most characteristic words of His gospel are " Fear not," " Do not worry." As He looked into men's hearts, He saw there a haunted world. Men were afraid of all kinds of things—the future and the past, the trouble that might come to-morrow, and the evil fruits of yesterday. They were afraid of one another, afraid of themselves. " If there were only one man in the world," said Goethe, " he would be a terror to himself." They were afraid of the Fates, even of God Himself as they knew Him. They were afraid of those who were their masters, of those also who were their slaves. They were afraid of changes, of

civil disturbance, of revolutions in religion,
of any kind of change in the old order of
things. They were afraid of death and the
afterward, and of all the nameless and in-
explicable and unpreventable suffering of
life. To Jesus, fear and care had the same
root. It was a wrong relation to God and
therefore to life : the evil could only be put
right by getting down to its roots and dealing
with it there. It was sheer atheism, however pure or worthy might be the motive
behind it ; a baptized unbelief, if you like,
sanctified by a lovingly anxious mind and a
high seriousness of purpose, but still unbelief.

And you find the same fear haunting the
world of to-day. How deeply the poison of
it is infecting our social life in every direction
we all know, breeding suspicion in all sorts of
ways, creating strife between man and man,
class and class, nation and nation. No social
solution for the ills of our common life is
going to be of any avail that does not eradi-
cate fear, by removing some of its prevent-
able and external causes. You find this fear
also in the individual conscience which still
" doth make cowards of us all." You find

it in relation to God and the religious outlook.   What a bankruptcy of any true vision
of God is revealed by our familiar superstitions; the pathetic dependence, for instance,
on mascots, which though apparently treated
as a joke, really mask for many people—
some of them professedly Christian—a super-
stitious outlook upon life.   What a chance
for a message about Providence and God's
ways with men and a truly religious attitude
to life, this provides for a preacher !   It may
seem a small thing that a man may dislike
sitting down one of thirteen at table, but you
have got a joint in his armour there, through
which you can reach his mind with a new
view of the universe and a new vision of God,
and release him from a whole battalion of
fears, of which he may have been unconscious, into a new freedom.   That is only
one illustration.   But in various ways fear
is operating, demanding security of material
kinds—the security of money or of armaments,
or of external authorities and ecclesiastically
guaranteed truth—in all of which, of course,
there is no real security but only, as Christ
often pointed out, another breeding-ground

for further fear. When we preach our gospel, we have to take account of fear.

Another element in man's nature is *pride*, which also takes many forms and makes the heart very sensitive at certain points. There is the pride that shows itself in social ostracism of others who are down, or of those who are supposed to be inferior. There is the pride that manifests itself in the easily offended spirit, and the subtle pride which demands a religion of good works. Pride sometimes issues also in a remorse that looks very Christian and may be really very un-Christian : the root of it is the refusal to accept oneself and the situation one has created, and the low estimate of our character which moral failure has brought, and demands instead a reinstatement to self-respect on the terms of some kind of self-justification and not of the forgiving light of truth and love. A great deal of pride, of course, is due to fear—the secret fear that we are not as good as we ought to be, or are not so sure of ourselves as we think we are, and therefore we compensate for this sense of inferiority by censoriousness or depreciation of others, or even by determined good works. It is easy to see what an opening for the gospel one can find at the sensitive point of pride, as it constantly offers itself to our attack.

Class distinctions and social barriers, these also Christ saw to be wrong with His world. Men had a wrong outlook to one another as individuals, as classes, as nations. The air was thick with prejudices. The great cleavage between the Jew and the Gentile illustrates some of them. A false patriotism created one barrier. The Jew had not learned the lesson taught by the great prophets and by that unknown genius who wrote the story of Jonah, that the place of privilege is a place of responsibility, and that the only aristocracy among nations and men is the quality of the service they are fitted to give to the world. There were barriers too between the classes, between master and slave, between the imperialist race and the subject people, between the religiously respectable and the outcast. You can see how Christ is always trying to break them down in parable after parable—the

Good Samaritan, the Pharisee and the Publican; the greatest story in all the world, the story of the Prodigal and the Elder Brother. These barriers were always creating sore spots which He attacked in His message, and found them often ready for the healing surgery of truth.

There is no need to point out that these barriers exist to-day, standing in the way of the gospel and blinding spiritual perception. Yet such is the reaction of evil that they provide a point at which we can bring men face to face with God. How easily men find their way into the secret of Jesus when these barriers are down, you can see in the case of the centurion. His openness to the glory of Jesus is explained just by the fact that, in his case, all the barriers were down. He had somehow overcome them all—the race barrier, the ecclesiastical barrier, the barrier of superiority which attaches to people of a dominant race, the barrier between officer and servant—they were all down. There was about the man a fine catholicity, and this openness to whatever was good in humanity laid him open

at once to the wonder of Jesus Christ. We
cannot enough appreciate how much these
barriers are hiding God. As we shall discover, the thing that is keeping many people
out of the Kingdom of God is just something
wrong somewhere in their relations with
another ; it may be in the home, it may be
in business, it may be as part of a race or
national prejudice which they share with
their fellows. In many a life it is just some
grudge, some wrong attitude, some bitter
memory, some twisted relationship, that is
holding up a great enlightening freedom.
Keep hold of this truth—the great door into
the Kingdom of God swings on some pivot in
the personal life of the man or woman with
whom you are dealing. People do not sur-
render to Christ in general or in the abstract.
The decisive step is never taken in the air, or
at least does not become effective until it
is embodied in some concrete thing. The
illuminating vision comes in the aspect of
some living situation which it reveals. Sometimes we recognize the coming of the light
only by the shadow which it throws. And
one of the commonest of the barriers that

5

hold the door in the lives of people is just the barrier between man and man. It is part of our great business to be reconcilers in ever so many ways, and among other reconcilements, to reconcile men to God by reconciling them to one another.

Yet another kind of trouble which Christ discerned and which gave the shape to much of His message was *false values*. The root of a good many troubles and sins is there. Take the incident of the man who came with his plea for justice in the division of some property. " Take heed," said Christ, " and beware of covetousness. For a man's life consisteth not in the abundance of the things which he possesseth." The man's values were wrong. The real trouble was the rift between him and his brother, but what was troubling him was that he was not getting enough money. He was looking at the latter as the chief thing in life, instead of brotherliness, as it was to Jesus, and this false valuation was introducing all kinds of jealousy and strife. How many quarrels would be settled out of hand if money took its rightful place—quarrels, too, which can

eventually be settled in no other way ! The
same is, of course, true of a dozen other things.
Even in many of our churches the average
man is all wrong in his standards—his
standards of greatness, of success in life, of
the real good and satisfaction of it. The
struggle of life grows hard and bitter because
our values are false in various directions.
Get right down to the social problem, to the
competition which turns life into a jungle for
both the fit and the unfit, and it is false
values that create the fever in the blood.
One of the keenest and most radical of our
Labour leaders was discussing with a group
of ministers what kind of message the Church
ought to be delivering to-day, and where lay
the real sore spot ; and he turned to them and
said something like this : " Your business,
gentlemen, is not with the economics or other
externals of the problem. Your business is
to change the standards of success." We
need only think for a moment to realize how
deep that suggestion cuts. The real thing
that makes life so miserably poor for some
and so miserably prosperous for others, is in
the standards of success which men have set

up for themselves ; or had forced upon them, as some have, by that bitter social struggle. If we can bring men to see that money is only valuable as a means of service, that true success consists in the kind of manhood we are building up, that real joy is found along the pathway of unselfishness, that persons are worth more than property, we shall have created the atmosphere in which alone any true reconstruction of society becomes possible. To change men's values means to change everything for them—their interests, their desires, their ambitions ; it is in very truth the gift of a new heart.

And, last of all, the trouble of life is rooted in *religious unreality*. There were many excellent people among the religious folk of Palestine, as we know—many excellent people among the Pharisees. We can never forget that the temper of the race from which they sprang was that which sharpened the swords of the early Maccabees. But the trouble was that religion had become hardened into formula and ritual. Men who have to fight for a religious principle embodied in some creed, or ritual, or method of worship, nearly always tend to stereotype their religion in that external thing, forgetting the principle and making the formula everything, losing the living spirit and sanctifying the ritual act or institution. Ritual becomes everything — the heart, nothing ; the temple, everything—the God who is everywhere, forgotten ; the altar, supreme—the love and the surrendered will, nothing ; virtue or sin in the act, everything—the intention or the living will behind the act, nothing. Who shall say that Pharisaism is dead ? As a matter of fact, it is the second stage of a religious experience that has lost touch with its original impulse. Part of our great business to-day is to bring men face to face with the living spirit. What is religious reality ? It is that attitude to God as personal holy love which finds expression through everything. It finds and seeks expression in ritual postures and praises, only that it may the more definitely and clearly keep that attitude in the daily work and relationships of life. Worship is only real when there is no contradiction in any of its acts or ritual, with our real relationship to God.

Love to God is only real when it finds expression in love to men, its only medium.
It is of no use a man calling Christ "Lord"
who does not do the thing which He com-
mands. It is mere mockery to recite a
creed which is not the utterance of a joyful
and convincing experience. To bring reality
back into religion by helping men to find
afresh, and have ever recreated within them,
the living experience ; to tear off masks
which men put on to hide from the reality of
their own condition, or the reality of a love
and forgiveness which they can get on no
other terms than by a Father's mercy—that
is part of our task in preaching. But here,
again, we can find a foothold for our message
in extraordinary ways. There are people in
all our churches to whom your message along
this line will be hard and distasteful in the
extreme. But there are others who are longing for a right release from some burden of
religious observances which is galling them,
but which they cannot give up because they
are held to these observances by holy associations, or because they feel they ought to find
in them the joy and peace which they are

seeking there. You will bring them release if you will first help them frankly to face the fact that they find nothing in these observances and then open up for them that new contact with the Father by which the old wells once more are bubbling with living water. What a field for preaching on prayer, on worship, on the Sacrament of the Lord's Supper ; reinterpreted in the light of our true relation to God the Father, and restored to a living medium of His intercourse with His children, and of their intimate brotherhood with one another !

II

So far I have been speaking of what might be termed the negative elements in human nature—the things that make our problem, and create what we call sin. For all acts of sin more or less proceed from these deep roots. This brings me to say that it is no use preaching against sin in general. There is no such thing, in the abstract ; any more than there is any such thing as goodness in the abstract. The fact that people are not worrying about their sins, to use a phrase

that became threadbare long ago, is really
very largely due to the fact that our conceptions of sin have been often just as unreal as our conceptions of goodness—a series
of conventional acts which had little obvious
relation to our attitude to God as His children.
Most of the " sins of society," as they are
called, can only be rightly seen as sins and
convincingly condemned in the light of great
principles which would equally condemn
things that the ordinary man never thinks
of calling sin.   It is along these lines we can
" convince the world of sin."   But that is
to anticipate what I propose to deal with
later on.

Let me now for a little, touch on the more
positive elements in the hearts and minds
of men, which are our allies in bringing men
to God.   Two illusions, I believe, are shattered
for many people by the experience of the
last few years, or will need to be shattered
by our message.   One is the mechanical
idea of progress.   The notion that there is
such a thing as a river or stream of progress
that somehow carries us along if only we will
just drift and so somehow " get better and

better every day" or every century, is gone
for ever. The other illusion is the belief in a
magical Christianity. The latter, I know,
dies hard, and in some quarters it is fighting
desperately for its life and making a brave
show of vitality ; but, generally speaking,
sensible men are not now repeating so much
as formerly the shibboleth that " Christianity
has failed," a phrase that really reflects a
belief in some magical Christianity. The
shattering of these illusions has, with many,
only produced despair — despair of any
progress, or of any power in the Christian
faith, or of any help in God. But, on the
other hand, with many there is a growing
realization that God can help us, but only in
the measure of the response of our whole
personality, mind and heart and will, to
His adventure of seeking, saving love. And
there are many who are really asking, " What
must we do to be saved ? "—or as a young,
alert man put it to me once, " How do you
get going in this business ? " with the
assurance that whatever it meant, he was
in for it with his whole self.

There is an eagerness, a wistfulness, abroad

in the world to-day. There is, for instance, the demand for some view of life that shall give it meaning and make sense of existence. Many people are looking at the world as F. W. H. Myers looked at the Sphinx, with one question which they long to ask, " Is the universe friendly ? " It will be your business to do for them what the princess in Turganev's story did for herself. Her lover had given her a ring with a carved Sphinx upon it, to typify the strange conflict in her which he could not understand. After some years it was sent back to him, and he found she had scratched across the figure of the Sphinx, the form of a Cross. You will have to show men how it is in the Cross that the meaning of life is found.

Further, people to-day are in many cases not only longing for some purpose in life that is big enough to explain it to the satisfaction of their minds ; it must also be intelligible enough and practical enough for them to lay hold of it, and so to lay hold of it that it will take up every movement of their being and express the true selfhood which is the hidden urge of every personality. We can hardly over-estimate what a secret curse to many a man and woman is the sense of futility in life. You will find it in the most unlikely quarters. The want of a purpose in life is at the root of half the cases that visit the psycho-analysts. Many of the younger people, whatever they may appear to be on the surface, are seeking some task which will give them three things, as I heard it once put : " A definite purpose in life, a medium of expressing the unselfish instincts of their nature, a part to play in stemming the tide of human suffering." Every one may not be able to put it so clearly or even be conscious that such divine fires of longing are burning within. But it is part of our business as preachers to bring to consciousness and put into definite form, these shadowy yearnings after God—for that is what they are. We can be sure of this, people are waiting for that self-revealing and for the message that shall both awaken and fulfil.

Then there is the sense of moral failure. People may not know what sin is, because we have so often switched the idea of it on to some side-track of lurid vice. But they

know what moral failure is. Life with its
high demands has crippled them, because on
any high view of it, it is too much for us, if
we try to live it without God. Sooner or
later, something crashes through the shelters
of self-esteem and self-sufficiency, and gives
men and women a shuddering look into the
depths. Sometimes it is just when they go
out on that road of a great purpose, and find
they cannot keep their feet on it, that they
come at last to confess that while much is
wrong with the world which they long to
put right, something is also wrong with
them, and that they must begin with the
cosmos by beginning at home. Are not our
very philanthropies to-day, our passion for
social service, leading to something like a
realization of spiritual bankruptcy? Signs
are not wanting in that direction. When a
woman who begins by leading the feminist
movement ends by becoming an enthusiast
for the second advent, it is a sign at least of
moral despair which can only be met through
some vision of God. There are other cases
still more significant. Even if it be despair
which is the real significance of the second

coming movement—as it often is—it is a significant despair, for it means a recognition that without spiritual forces which are supernatural, there is no real headway to be made against evil enmeshed in a social system which it has created. Many of the best men in the Labour movement are beginning to have at least a fear that there is not idealism enough in the movement to run it and keep it together : there is even a wistfulness in many hearts nearly approaching an open ear.

There is more than a wistfulness in some hearts. There is a real sorrow before which all the shelters are down. Something in the heart of every man cries out for " a great companion," but the solitude in which we really live does not appear till sorrow makes it awesomely audible—a silence which can be felt. We can be sure of this—there is a conspiracy in life to bring men to the need of God. That is the very way in which we can truly speak of God being in our disciplines ; they all come out of a love which, in creating the universe of free beings, so made it that no man through the abuse of his freedom would put himself for ever beyond the reach of that love. But rather, so sinking, he would come upon the need of it and find himself open to it on some other level. " O God, my barque is so small, and Thy ocean is so great." That cry of the Breton fisherman lies waiting, unspoken, for something which sooner or later will set it free in a prayer, and our business is to be ready for that moment, even though we should be tempted sometimes to despair of its ever arriving.

In all sorts of hearts too, there is the hope, often disguised, that God will do something. It may be disguised as a kind of shallow optimism, which we will have to reinterpret; or it may appear as the cult of the second coming or some such doctrine, which has a great hope in it as well as a despair. Some one the other day even described the gambling fever as " the prostitution of hope!" But in broken hearts and down in the depths there still is hope—the conviction that somehow God has control of the situation which man has mishandled, and that some day there will be a clearing up.

Whether men be conscious of God or not,

whether they have any kind of religious outlook or not, one thing is sure. God is in the life of every man in some kind of spiritual experience ; unrecognized it may be, but present. " He has not left Himself without a witness." To interpret God's dealings with us in the things which men feel sacred, is our task. The thing we need to do for a great many people in our day—serious people, the " godless good," as the *Spectator* once called them, and people who are not conscious of any goodness at all—is to bring them to recognize God, who is already at work in their lives. That is the hope and wonder of our life in the ministry, that we are dealing with men and women in whose hearts, all unknown, God is at work in ways which we can discover and make known to them ; so that experience, however commonplace it seems, becomes lustrous with the Divine ; only a thin door and the uplifting of a latch is between them and the Friendship which is the glory and the worth of life.

One of the needs of to-day is, I repeat, to help men to realize that religion is natural ; that when a man comes to himself, he prays and turns to His Father ; and conversely, that when he comes to terms with God, he comes to himself. Nothing can be more discouraging than to picture the religious experience in terms that put it beyond the conception or the reach of a natural healthy man. Goodness is natural, faith is natural, fellowship with God is natural, or it is hopeless. It is something, to quote Dr. T. R. Glover, that can be achieved by a man with a wife and five children. But this is to trench on what I want to say later. When Marco Polo, the great traveller, came home to Venice he knocked at the door of his relatives' house—an old man, travel-stained, with an old cloak over his shoulders. They did not recognize him, and saw nothing more in him than a far-travelled stranger who needed hospitality, and out of their goodness of heart they took him in and set him down with them at table. For a while he talked and entertained them with his interesting discourse. Then he flung off the old dust-stained cloak, and beneath it disclosed a garb of richest silk brought from the far-away lands, whilst from his wallet he drew

gifts of jewels and precious stones, rare
spices and costly ivory. And on a sudden
they found that he was not only their long-
lost friend, but also their benefactor, enrich-
ing life beyond their dreams. That is the
deepest need of men, to find in their experience what has been theirs all the time in
kindly love and gracious inspirations ; and
various kinds of moral challenge begin to
grow through Christ into a living fellowship
with a loving Father, in whom they really
live and move and have their being. To
find in their own experience the key to this
redeeming discovery, and put it into the
hands of men, is part of the task and the
joy of preaching.

It may seem as if, in thus analysing the
preacher's audience with such care as scope
permits, I have left out the most important
part of it—those, namely, who are already in
the Kingdom, and who will come to us for
instruction and for help. God forbid that I
should forget them, or that any of us in our
preaching should forget them—the people who
walk with God. To do so is a defect into
which the savage criticism of the Church,

6

which passes with many for prophetic zeal, may lead us in our youth. We will learn in time that this is one of the real privileges of the ministry—to " minister to the saints " in deed and in truth. Among them you will find an eagerness for fresh truth, a kindling of the eye, a rare faculty of appreciation, though it be only in one here and there or in a little group, which will make you feel when they are absent as if you were preaching to an empty church. They are always seeking to learn. Our constant humiliation will be the thought that they are willing and hopeful to learn of us, winnowing the grain from the chaff of our immaturities. But even with some of these the whole connotation of the saved life needs reminting, " for time makes ancient good uncouth." Even the saints, who like the holy families of Israel, wait for the consolation of God and His appearing, need to realize that He only breaks in through our ever-growing vision of Him in Christ and our response to what we see. Even *they* need to realize that conversion means thinking with the mind of Christ about everything, that what Christ did for us only becomes effective in the measure in which it enables us to do the same for others. There are those to whom the Cross is the height of all wonders, constantly taking their hearts with love and, as with Bunyan's Christian, sending " the waters that are in their heads down their cheeks " for gratitude. But even these need to discover that emotion is not salvation, and that we are only redeemed according as our lives become redeeming. It is a hard journey we may have to take them, but at least our comfort is that many are waiting and willing to be led.

LECTURE III

SOME TYPES OF PREACHING

FROM one point of view it is as impossible to classify types of preaching as it is impossible, except very generally, to classify types of men. Preaching is essentially the impression of one personality upon others. However varied the subject, a man's own outlook, his point of view, the subtle essence of his own spirit, will out. "The teacher's heart," says Emerson, "cannot be hid." Consequently every man will have his own note, his own interest, which will appear in his preaching. The most we do for a congregation, even after years of service, is to give them a point of view from which to look at life and think of God. In point of fact, that is what we should strive most of all to give them ; for if we have not helped them to think for themselves and judge for themselves, we have not greatly succeeded. Dean

Inge, in an address to teachers, said the true teacher's business was to make the pupil independent of him. This is true of the preacher as well. A congregation may " sit at our feet," as the saying has it, but we must not forget that their prime business is to walk upon their own. Only as we help them to that, are we really helping them. The best minister is the man who makes his people less and less dependent on himself, because he has been helping them to make their own contacts with the mind of Christ.

Generally speaking, there are three dominant interests in the preaching outlook which are represented by types of preaching. They are the evangelistic, the ethical, and the doctrinal. It is worth while to think of these in turn, though they cannot well be separated from each other. A good evangelistic sermon, for instance, will be ethical in its direction and doctrinal in its foundations : whilst, as we would all agree, ethics without the evangel is machinery without power ; and without doctrine, out of any real relation with a reasonable universe, making duty a mere irrational intruder, a Pied Piper with an undeniable call, but leading, for all we could know, only to the abyss. It was F. W. H. Myers who wrote :

" Whoso hath felt the Spirit of the Highest,
    Cannot confound or doubt Him or deny."

But it was Myers also who forsook the Christian position because, he said, Christ had no cosmic significance. Preaching, whatever the particular emphasis of one sermon or another, must have in it all three elements.

Yet throughout the course of the preaching ministry, there will be a place for each of these three kinds of preaching. If there is one thing more than another we must beware of, it is becoming stereotyped in our choice of subjects. We are all prone more or less to the peril of the closed mind ; or the mind so nearly closed that there is only a gateway for a certain order of ideas, all others being mechanically excluded by the law of interests. Many people maintain a rigid censorship of unfamiliar ideas, and the preacher is not exempt from this defect. For all his wide reading he as well as others may have a closed mind.

It is not merely reading, by the way, that

will save us from this defect, but the habit of taking time to think. We may read many books and never see anything in them but what is cognate to one narrow circle of ideas. We are in the zone of danger in this respect whenever we find in our reading only illustrations of what we know already. Many of us read too much and think too little; and even in what we read, amid the pressing work of the ministry it is so easy to get into the way of only reading books that lie comfortably to the set of our minds and neglect the books that take us out of the depths in which we feel safe. There are no rules which can be laid down. Each man must find his own way. A man with one of the freshest theological minds in this country told me that he reads hardly anything except his Bible, which I imagine is the exact inversion of the methods of many people.

It is a good thing for the sake of our people, as well as for our own self-discipline, to look back now and then on the course our preaching has taken during the previous month or two, on the ground we have covered, and on the range of subjects we have been dealing

with, to make sure that unconsciously we
have not been slipping into a rut. And we
should make sure of room and space in our
programmes for sermons which are in their
emphasis devoted to each of these three kinds
of preaching, for they correspond to definite
parts of the preacher's aim, and to definite
aspects of God in Christ, and of that relation
to Himself into which He seeks to bring us.

I

Let us think first of all of what is called
evangelistic preaching. We cannot define it
so as to please every one. I remember spending three Sunday evenings in succession
trying " to do the work of an evangelist," as
the Scripture has it, and proposed so to spend
a fourth evening, when I received a letter
from a stranger telling me he had been worshipping in my congregation for three weeks
and had been edified more or less, but he had
one favour to ask—Would I kindly preach
the gospel for once before he left ! Evangelistic preaching is presenting Christ to men
in such a way as to win them into a personal
love and loyalty to Him. There are many

forms of what is called the evangelical experience, but there is only one evangelical experience, whatever shape it may take or whatever emotional accompaniments may attend its birth. That experience is the awakening of personal faith in Jesus Christ as Saviour, Leader, Master, Friend—use whatever words of personal human relationship we may in which to define it : they are all mirrors of that experience. That personal contact with Christ is the burning centre of our religion. It is only in this experience that our relation to God as personal Father is brought to a focus point in reality ; and only in this experience can our nature as His children be harmonized and the soul be set moving on the way of its true independence and proper freedom.

How is this experience to be awakened ? Only by such preaching as reveals Christ in His life, His spirit, His attitude to men and women, His contacts with people of all kinds and conditions of need, and centrally in His Cross. The heart of the whole message, of course, is there. " The great offensive of love," as it has been called, comes to a head there in all its elements of righteousness, faith, and compassionate forgiveness. There also where love meets the opposition of men, their fear, their pride, their false values, their lovelessness, their religious unreality — all these blinding elements of man's estrangement from God, in the Cross come to a head in a vividness which can reach the most hardened heart to unveil it. But we must not forget that while the Cross is, as it were, the point where the rays of God's love in Christ are focussed, that love shines through the life and spirit of Christ at every point, for the Cross is interpretative of the constant activity of Jesus toward men all through. The Cross must never be preached as a mere symbol or as some magic talisman. It is Jesus who is there revealed Who must be preached ; and the way of love revealed in the Cross shown to be characteristic of His Spirit all through. At every point in the life of Christ you touch the infinite love in action : sometimes in the smallest and most trivial thing. Hence evangelistic preaching may be defined as preaching Jesus so that *He* stands revealed. It is telling the story in such a way that people see Him as He is. It is, as it were, flinging on the screen of the mind and imagination the pictures of Christ which are in the gospel story in miniature. We have to preach Christ—not preach about Christ, and there is here a real distinction. A good deal of preaching is preaching about Christ in such a way that He becomes merely a kind of symbol of God, and not in His own person a living reality who meets men and in whom men meet God.

Many a faithful preacher searching his habitual message for the possible secret of its failure has found it here. He has been speaking much about Jesus, but He Himself has never been disclosed to make His own appeal. It is practically useless, in an age which knows little of Jesus from its own reading of the Scriptures, to ask men to look at Him or think of Him. There are some perhaps to whom it is enough to utter the Name for a vivid picture of Him, which is already in the background of consciousness to spring into life and stand before them. But there are many others to whom He is but a name, without much more than a misty content. It is not our business to argue about Him, or defend Him, or even state the need for Him, but to preach Him. He alone can do His own work in bringing men to Himself, and that only in the measure in which He is revealed. When we have something to show people which is worth looking at, we do not need to beg them to look at it. We throw a light upon it which enables it to become its own attraction. " I, if I be lifted up," He said, " will draw all men unto Me " ; it is a word which, like many more of His words, is capable of suggesting a variety of meanings, of which none is without significance ; and this is one, that the key to success in evangelistic preaching is our ability to set forth Jesus.

We are the more tempted to this kind of preaching nowadays because there is a big hiatus in many minds between Christ and God, and we soon begin to feel the need of removing it. This is best dealt with in a sermon which is more particularly doctrinal. But let us remember that the bridge is not capable of being built till Christ is so revealed that men find God in Him ; and they find God in Him through what He was and is, in His person and life in relation to men. If He is truly preached, Jesus will create for people His own theological significance, and there is no other way of helping people to find God in Him, except by the revelation of the Divine in His nature as holy forgiving love. We must help people to see Jesus. Everything begins there. And what better material can we have than the numberless stories which reveal Christ in His contacts with men and women — the story of Zacchæus, the woman at the well, the healing miracles, the woman who was a sinner ; in His dealings with the disciples in some moment of their perplexity or impotence ; in parables like the Prodigal Son, the Good Samaritan, and the like, revealing the love of God in the human relations of people who acted like Him. We cannot read the Book of Acts, especially its early chapters, without realizing that the dynamic thing is contact with a living Christ—a Christ personally real in His moral demand and His individualizing love, and immediate in His touch with men and women and His guidance of their lives. It is true the phrase—" the living Christ "—is suspect to-day, partly for the associations which cling to it and partly because people are perplexed about it, and we will need to be able to deal with people for whom the centuries are an impassable barrier.

> " Dim tracts of time divide
> These golden days from me.
> Thy voice comes strange o'er years of change,
> How can I follow Thee ? "

We will need to be prepared to deal with that aspect of unreality, and we can help many thinking people if we offer them a way of seeing the immediacy of their own personal spiritual relation to Christ. And the only way is by preaching Christ so as to awaken the sense of His own spiritual and personal reality. The preaching of Christ, as He is, can bring people so into vital relation with Him that their trouble is not how they can conceive the possibility of finding touch with Him through the centuries, but how along the corridors of any universe they can escape from Him.

The best way, on the whole, is to take it for granted that Jesus meets men to-day, and go on to reveal Him. No man can get face to face with Christ without being brought into a world in which space and time are transcended. That is His power. You cannot finally explain it, or argue men into the reality of Jesus. You can only bring it home by revealing Him so that He produces His own immediate impression of an authoritative and irresistible love. When Romola was fleeing from Florence because things had become too much for her, she suddenly came face to face with Savonarola, who at once bade her return. "She started up," says George Eliot, "with defiant words ready to burst from her lips, but they fell back without utterance. She had met his calm glance, and the impression of it was so new to her that her anger sank back as something irrelevant. The source of the impression his glance produced was the sense it conveyed of interest in her and care for her. . . . It was simple human fellowship expressing itself as a strongly felt bond." That is the kind of impression which Jesus can produce — the impression of interest and care, of human fellowship rising into a personal bond—the

love which will neither let us off nor let us
go. And that bond is the saving—the
evangelical—thing.

There are problems connected with evangelism. It has its own dangers. The
motives we urge and the appeals we make
must all be in the line of the message of Jesus.
That is quite clear. No man can be really
bound to Christ by motives that are not
Christian. Is it legitimate to use the appeal
of fear? In the old way, certainly not.
Any psychologist will tell you that there is a
real danger in an appeal which plays upon
the vague and indefinite fears that are a
part of the mental inheritance of many
people.

On the other hand, there are many states
of anxiety from which it is the work of the
gospel to deliver men, because they proceed
from ourselves or rise, it may be, from some
wrong thought of God. And when they are
faced in the light of Jesus they will vanish.
It will be found, perhaps as Bunyan's pilgrim
found, that the lions which looked so terrible
are chained, or, on the other hand, that like
the Brocken spectre they are only the pro-

jection of our own selves upon a world on which the sunlight has not risen. If people have fears relating to a spiritual condition or an external circumstance they must be helped to face them in the light of truth, not to escape from them by any retreat into a vague or sentimental idea of God's goodness or His forgiveness. The gospel must never be proclaimed as a shelter from self-judgment or from the external consequences of sin ; the real consequences of sin in the blinded conscience and in the moral nature incapacitated for goodness and the fellowship of God, are the things from which Christ came to deliver us. But it must be made clear that true peace is only found in the presence of a love from which we have nothing left in us to hide, whose very quality is of light in which everything is revealed, and which makes us glad to have it so. The message needed by those who are afraid of external consequences is just that of a love which is able to make us face them without fear.

And yet is there nothing which we ought legitimately to fear ? Will not true evan-

7

gelical preaching strive to awaken the vision
of Christ and of life in Him, and so to
awaken it that the thought of missing it,
and of the sin through which we miss it, will
send a shudder through the soul? The one
thing men dare healthily fear is to lose the
life in Christ and our true relation to God in
Him, for the real content of that fear is the
fear of evil and lovelessness.

The question of evangelism naturally also
brings up the question of emotion. What
is the place of emotion in preaching? Some
one says that we may well suspect an
emotion in preaching which we do not feel in
the study in preparing the message. There is
truth in that. Yet surely there are levels
of significance which the truth opens up in
the act of preaching which might not have
appeared when we prepared the message.
Emotion there must be. It is a vital part of
the response of our whole self to the truth.
It will come naturally in apprehending the
truth we are proclaiming. If there be no
emotion there, something will be wrong
with our vision of the truth. All response
to truth is a response in part of some kind of

feeling. But the truth and the clear vision of it in all its meanings must be the dominant thing for life. To work up emotion as some do because in reality they have a lurking scepticism about the power of the truth is not only useless ; it is degrading, unreal, only a superior kind of force. One has seen a congregation literally held up and its pockets picked by a sentimental appeal for charity which was positively harmful ; it awakened no real thought or concern for those who were suffering, such as would bring the audience into a real relation to them as members one of another and so help to change the situation. It merely produced the feeling that a donation would discharge their liability. Nothing will create so much the feeling of unreality as the effort to be impressive. If our *message* is not impressive we may make any other kind of impression we like ; it will not be a spiritual impression. The young people of the last generation might have been impressed by it, though not religiously ; most young people to-day will smile. Nothing is so difficult to conceal from the latter as stage mechanism

danger of the old preaching was that religion
should divorce ethics ; the danger of the new
kind of preaching is that ethics should divorce
religion.   What is the practical connection
between them so far as we are concerned with
it in our preaching ?   It may be put in this
way—that all conduct is the vital medium
of a man's relation with God the Father as
His child.   In other words, we are not religious
in order to help us to be good, but we are good
in order to be truly religious.   Goodness is
incomplete ; it has no real meaning, save as it
is the material, the sacramental medium, of
a man's fellowship with God ; and with God
through fellowship with man.   Beware, with
all your power, of the kind of preaching which
would merely reduce God to the level of an
ally of man in the maintenance of his own
self-respect or his own ideal of righteousness.
The immediate effect of such preaching is to
produce the conception of a God whom many
people in this age do not feel they need ; and
many others, if they would confess it, do not
regard as having any power.   Till conduct,
as the science of right relations of man with
man, becomes for us part of our personal

attitude to God, we have not discovered our real power either to advocate the good or to condemn the evil.

Why is anything good or bad? We have got to face that question. Why should people not break the Ten Commandments? That is what they are asking to-day, and we have little to say to them unless we relate their lives to God in Christ Jesus, and to that thought of man and society and the world which is bound up with the Christian outlook. There is a drift from the old moorings which is not going to be arrested by mere denunciations from the pulpit or by any attempt to recapture the thunders of Sinai. We will have to deal in the pulpit with some of the big vices — drunkenness, immorality, gambling. But these cannot be dealt with merely by direct intention, or in isolation, or by devoting special sermons to them, though that must be done occasionally. We will, by the way, not find anything better than a course on the Ten Commandments, and we will discover if we try to preach on them that they contain a good deal of positive doctrine, and give us a good basis for reconstructing morality on the principles of Jesus. But the point I want to make is this, that we cannot condemn a thing like, for instance, gambling, or any other vice, except by reference to principles which will condemn our life at many other points, and again and again will lay low in the dust the respectable conventions of many who point the finger at the publican and sinner. Only in the light of the principles which proceed from the message of God and our true relation to Him and to His children, can we hope to awaken the sense of sin.

Another subject that will call for attention is the ethics of the home, the relations of parents to their children and *vice versa*. You will be surprised to find how often the real hindrance to religious feeling and faith is there. A young man's conflict with his father, or a girl's with her mother, in many cases chokes the spring. The sane and penetrating spirit of Christian relations works out in the ethics of the New Testament. " Children, obey your parents in the Lord." " Parents, provoke not your children to anger lest they be discouraged." No moral reform needs so much attention, and will mean so much for religion and for the world, as the Christianizing of home relationships. How little parents understand that they mediate God the Father to their children on the one hand, training them for fellowship with God, and on the other that there is a point where their authority must rightly give way in order that the higher authority of the perfect Father may be realized. A true apprehension of God's relation to us would cast a flood of light on home-life that would change its whole character and prevent numberless mistakes.

Preaching must also, of course, deal with the ethics of our social relations. A man is not Christian till he is concerned with the case of his brother in all sorts and conditions of need. No one can apprehend the teaching of Jesus without seeing that persons count for more than property, and that we are all more or less responsible for one another. And no one can look with Christian eyes on the world to-day without seeing how these principles are outraged. Whatever view we may take of any alternative, our present system of competition is seamed with iniquities. Our present social and industrial order offers a challenge to the Church as to its faith in the Lordship of Jesus. The same thing is true of our international relationships. Part of our task is to create a public conscience with regard to war as a method of settling disputes, and to develop the idea underlying the League of Nations. We have got to change the whole associative value of the word patriotism. As it is familiarly used it is not Christian, and just there lies half the trouble of the world. A large part of our message, then, will have to deal with our social, industrial, and international life. But we will find that much of the trouble in these is really rooted in various kinds of wrong attitudes of people to one another which exist in what are called private relations and even in the Church. It is perfectly appalling how unchristian people can be toward one another—and that even without knowing it— because our social conventions are poisoned with false valuations of personality. And preaching will have to deal with that. But one thing ought to be said. The worst way of treating these problems is by a continuous policy of indignant condemnation : that is, a preaching that only raises a blister on the skin and never gets down to the real disease. We will have to point out the anomalies, the injustices, the things in the world, where all men are God's children, that must break the heart of the Father and deny the spirit of love. We will have to quicken conscience, and show that there is no salvation for any man which does not take him out of selfishness into the lives of others. But do not let us forget that there are countless people in positions of responsibility and privilege who long to find a right solution of the problems, and feel nearly powerless. Certain kinds of preaching fill them with despair because they do not suggest one single thing which they can do except come out of the world altogether and give up business or do something else which would cause endless confusion. They are anxious for guidance. Surely there must be a really Christian way for them to follow now in their present situation, even amid the anomalies that belong to an industrial system not yet fully Christianized. They are asking for help, and it is our business to help them, and to sympathize with them in their difficulties. How in these days is a man to be a Christian workman, a Christian employer, a Christian foreman, a Christian shopkeeper, a Christian stockbroker, a Christian captain of industry, a Christian clerk? For in the long run, the key of the position depends on people seeing the light in their own situation, and following it step by step. The better world comes into being by the creation of the Christian mind in every kind of man and his loyalty to it in his own situation. The new world begins there.

The worst possible attitude for a preacher is that of a "Daniel come to judgment." We have no right to ally ourselves with any one class in the community to the exclusion of our sympathy with others. Materialism and selfishness are not the prerogatives of any one class. The gospel of Christ in its total message will in some ways be as distasteful to King Demos as it is to King Crœsus. All great changes come from within the individual. "Be ye transformed by the renewing of your mind," says Paul. Our chief business in this direction is with the mind of a converted man. We have to help people to realize the ethical nature of all Christian experience—that we cannot love God fully save through our love of men, or serve Him save through our service of one another ; that worship in the Church means an attitude to God the Father of His children which must be maintained in all our attitudes to life and to one another throughout the week ; that the Christian way of life must penetrate our corporate relationships ; that hatred is wrong wherever it is found ; that force achieves no lasting spiritual result ; that only a spiritual advance makes progress ; that a man is not converted till he is thinking with the mind of Jesus about everything, and is walking in the light he sees. That kind of ethical preaching is, to my thinking, the only kind which is of use.

It is one thing to knock Dagon from his throne, another thing to put the ark of God in his place. It is one thing to search conscience with the fire of our own hard judgments, another thing to turn upon the evil the light of God's love. Our business is not only to be the instruments of the clean heart, but also the medium of the right spirit, without which the clean heart cannot be permanent—if indeed it can be achieved at all. The parable of the empty house is warning enough against a merely external reformation conducted by force or fear. Whatever we are able to do as preachers must be done in the region of the total attitude to life. If we can achieve a quickened conscience alive and restless, and with it such a sense of life's true values in Christ as shall bring the spirit of detachment from position and possession, we shall have done a mighty thing in the region of Christian ethics. We shall have prepared the way of the Lord.

III

But now let us pass on to think of doctrinal preaching. One gathers from many sources that the modern reaction against doctrinal preaching is somewhat abating. The war has done one sound thing at least in this region. It has revealed the need for a reconstructed view of the universe and for some clear, intelligent conception of God which can meet the challenge of a world in ruins. We have got to help our people into a theology. We have got to help them to think. Democracy, and Protestantism in the best sense of the word—two movements which we believe have God in them, and took their rise upon a Christian view of the valuation of personality and of God's way of helping men to be themselves—depend on minds which are willing to think for themselves, and will refuse the domination of either priest or demagogue whose passion is to keep grown men in the nursery. There are vague heresies in our day soaking down into the minds of ordinary people through various popular media, which we cannot meet without an intelligent and instructed Christianity. What do we mean by God ? By His power, His government, His providence ? Why is it really silly to touch wood when you have been boasting to people how long it is since you had influenza ? There is a whole wrong attitude to life cropping up in such simple superstitions which can only be met by a clear and reasonable view of God. And the age is very fruitful in superstition, which is

the revenge of faith for its neglect. Or,
again, what is the real nature of love, the
meaning of the Cross ? Why really did
Jesus die, and how can it possibly have any
relation to God's forgiveness ? And what is
forgiveness ? Why should we forgive our
enemies ? A whole range of theological
inquiry lies behind that last question. The
only final answer to the question of forgiveness demands a theology. Or, again, how
does God help us ? We simply cannot keep
the feet of certain people from straying into
the realm of magic in the search for God, until
we have helped them into a reasonable
doctrine of grace. People to-day are craving
for definite teaching. They are feeling the
need of a sound body of Christian doctrine.
Preachers who have tried the experiment
find that an audience of all ages and stages
of capacity will listen intently to a sermon
on the grace of God, or the meaning of
salvation, or the Divine omnipotence ; such
subjects as would make those who claim to
know " what the public want " shake their
heads and tell us how the pulpit is detached
from life. The question in the long run, of

course, is not what people want, it is what
they need.   A well-known picture-film artist,
in giving an account of his methods lately,
described how he made the experiment of
trying to meet the public taste, but finally
discovered that he had to follow his own
ideas even to create a popular success.
Many people do not know what they want,
and preaching merely shaped to their passing
moods would little satisfy them.   But deep
in their hearts there is the need for some
clear thought of God and of His ways with
us.   It is surprising, for instance, how often
people become bitter in trouble because they
think God sent it, and we must be able to
show them God's real relation to us amid
the sorrow and suffering of life.   A reasonable view of Providence is part of the gospel,
and may be, in point of fact, the way of
salvation for a mind held up, by some
snag of perplexity, from a whole-hearted
devotion to Christ.   Facts are not facts with
any meaning till they are seen in their
relations, and we cannot fully see Jesus, the
people who want Him without any theological entanglements notwithstanding, till

8

we see Him in the light of His universal
relationships.

It is just our suspicion of doctrine which
has led to the rise of such strange growths
as Christian Science, and to the popularity
of spiritualism. These would never have
attained their present proportions if it had
not been that some instinct which they represent has been denied its full satisfaction
in Christian teaching. There is a doctrine of
mental healing, of the connections between
the body and the mind, in a truly Christian
outlook. And we have missed it with our
wrong views of God's relation to pain and
suffering, and our false ideas of the duty of
resignation. A whole system of bad theology
lies behind the Christian Science movement ;
but it took its rise in protest against a defective system of Christian truth. The same
thing is true of spiritualism, now happily
losing its hold on the tortured minds of
people ; but the fact of its popularity points
clearly to the need of greater emphasis on
the doctrine of immortality.

Nothing will meet man's true need but a
doctrine which grapples with the facts of sin

and redemption.   We must not be afraid of
wide horizons.   It will often take the biggest
view of God we can preach to heal even a
trifling wound in some human heart.   But
two things should be kept in mind.   One is
that such doctrinal preaching must have the
savour and the salt of practical life.   Look
at the genius of Christ.   There is a whole theology implicit in the Parable of the Prodigal
Son.   There is enough in it to keep a preacher
going for half a winter.   There is not a
word in it but is alive with reality.   Doctrine
has got to be a philosophy of Christian fact
and experience which the people in front of
us can grasp because it is set forth in terms of
experience of their own.   And the simplest,
homeliest experience, as Jesus showed, is the
truest symbol of spiritual reality.   " In my
Father's   house   are   many   mansions " — a
picture like that, which belongs to simple
human life, has more in it of the elements of
reality, and can give a clearer conception of
Christian truth about immortality, than any
metaphysical reasonings.   It   contains   the
seeds of doctrine, but it belongs in its language
and symbolism to the realm of real experience.

missed something in our vision of the truth. Emerson says : " In that protest which each considerate person makes against the superstition of his times, he repeats step by step the part of the old reformers, and in the search for truth finds new perils to virtue. He learns again what moral vigour is needed to supply the girdle of a superstition. A great licentiousness treads on the heels of a reformation. ' Doctor,' said his wife to Martin Luther one day, ' how is it that whilst subject to papacy, we prayed so often and with such fervour, while now we pray with the utmost coldness and very seldom ? ' " The newer views, let us remember, will stand or fall by their power to produce the reality of the old experience to-day for life and the world. One wonders if that is not where many moderns fall short. Are we helping men to fear sin as once they feared hell ? Are we enabling them, with the modern views of the Atonement, to see the love of God in its redeeming passion, relating the Cross to man's deepest necessity in such a way as to recapture the music of the phrase—" He loved me, and gave Himself for me " ? A

traveller tells how in the heart of Africa he
met a college friend working as a missionary
—the last man he expected to see. "What
are you doing here?" he asked. "I came
to pay my debt," was the quiet answer.
Are we offering men the kind of gospel which
explains that?

We can only do our work of theological
reconciliation in the measure in which our
symbols of love—our theological windows—
can take in, so to speak, as much of the
real vision of God's love as the old. There
is no more pathetic plight than that of a
preacher standing between the message of
God and the needs of men, while the world,
or his own heart, is saying to him: "Sir, thou
hast nothing to draw with, and the well is
deep." In the last conversation which the
late Dr. P. T. Forsyth had with one of his
friends they spoke of our troubled age hunger-
ing for a vision of God. And Forsyth
suddenly broke out: "I would give more than
I can say," he said, "to get Spurgeon back
again—Spurgeon with all his intellectual
narrowness, but Spurgeon with his evangelical passion and his love-kindled heart."

We must be sincere with the truth. God has in our day shown us, and is continuing to show us, a way into a fuller and clearer light and a far more real religion than that of a generation ago. The truth will never fail us if we are loyal to it, and nothing but the truth will serve to help the world. The need is for clear thinking ; but also for thinking which is thorough and historically based. Tradition must not be our bond-slave ; the past experience of men must not be a chain. But we should beware lest, casting off tradition, we miss something to which it points, a light upon the face of Christ, seen and caught in some ancient formula, without which He cannot be in all His fulness, what He is—the light of all our modern day.

LECTURE IV

THE TECHNIQUE OF PREACHING

IT may argue a want of proportion to devote only one lecture to the subject of technique. But technique and method are largely dependent on other things—the preacher's grasp of his message and the spirit of the man. If these are right with us, our instinct will tend to lead us naturally to a right method. A man in dead earnest, with a life-and-death case to put, which is the true preacher's position, will feel his way to a right method. Through all kinds of imperfections of style and delivery, his message will get itself " across," to use a common word, while the most perfect technique with no kindled passion or lit mind behind it, will make of preaching no more than a moderately pleasant entertainment.

How independent Chalmers was of technique in certain directions ! Here is a description of his delivery from the pen of Dr. Caird. " No grandeur or dignity of person, no polish or refinement of speech or gesture, a voice without sweetness or melody and articulation thick or guttural, an accent not merely broadly Scottish but of undisguised provincialism ; instead of commanding and varied action following the changeful turns of thought and feeling, a continuous sawing of the air with one hand whilst the other followed the lines of a closely read manuscript. Such were the physical conditions which in the case of this orator seemed to render anything like eloquence impossible. Yet he broke through them all." And not only so, but when he preached in London two of the most polished orators in England, who were in his audience, confessed, " He beats us all." Needless to say, this is not cited for the relief of a tender artistic conscience, still less for our imitation. The worst possible style is one which imitates a defect or peculiarity in another whose genius or power has overcome it. Chalmers was Chalmers. The man was real through and through, and alive to the finger-tips with a message for his age. First things must come first. What we need most to-day is not a new preaching method or technique, but a new vision of the preacher's task and opportunity. That would produce on the most halting lips the gift of tongues.

But this is not to say that technique does not need attention. It needs it, just as much as a river channel needs to be cleared of snags and obstructions, and for a similar reason— that the truth may have " free course and be glorified." Anything on the one side or the other which draws attention to the preacher himself is a positive obstruction. The preacher whose style is so polished or whose technique is so impressive that people stop listening to his message to think of him, is in that measure an impediment to his own power. We can add nothing to the power of the truth by any effort of our own. All our efforts in the direction of style or delivery must be devoted to make our speech and method a clear channel for truth, a mirror whose main glory is to vanish in the light it reflects. No doubt you know the difference between an organist who is a real leader of praise and one who is a master of show effects. The one is a self-forgetful treasure ; the other is a self-conscious nuisance. The same thing may be true of a preacher. One of the worst effects of a bad style is that it keeps both preacher and people from a real sincerity. It produces a sense of strain and uneasiness in the atmosphere. The object of attention to method and technique should be to deliver both preacher and audience from consciousness of themselves and of one another, so that the message of God may become the dominating fact.

I

The first thing in sermon preparation is to get our subject. The subject may be contained in a text or an incident from Scripture ; or it may be found elsewhere, as, for instance, upon rare occasions, in some event of importance which is occupying the public mind : or in some poem or other literary work, though this also should only be upon occasion. I am not prepared to be dogmatic on the point, but I fear I can only admire at a distance the man who can find his subject

in secular literature. His purpose is to be
respected, which is to get hold of the man
who is more interested in, let us say modern
poetry, than he is in the Psalms of David ;
but the value of this method is very doubtful,
except as an occasional variation. It is
quite another thing, of course, when this is
done in a class of special people. The main
thing is our message, whatever our subject,
but in general we will find the latter in some
word or incident or book of Scripture. For
remember the Bible is still the authoritative
book on the Christian religion ! And we will
find, as we go on, that Scripture has this
peculiar and unique quality of inspiration,
that it plumbs depths which the human
soul, even in the most profound of other
literature, has never exceeded, while it em-
bodies its experience in phrases and ex-
pressions which are final, even from the
literary point of view.

How do texts come ? Nothing can take
the place of the study of Scripture ; our
business is to know the Bible. There will
be little difficulty about finding subjects on
which to preach if we are faithful to our

continuous study of the Scriptures. But a message often leaps at us from the reading and meditation which we do for our own spiritual culture. The best texts often come to us like other best things, when we are not directly seeking them. Life's dealings with ourselves, as we seek in Scripture to find light for our own path, will break the envelope which wraps many a precious message, and do it better than anything else. The word men want to hear from us is the word which, through our own experience, God is speaking to ourselves. The message which is minted in the crucible of our own need alone bears the stamp of reality. Or, again, we may find our text suggested to us by some concrete case we have met with as our hearts are open to the sorrows and sins of others. That is really the same thing, for a Christian minister's experience has, more than other men's, a vicarious element. We will be constantly up against questions which people are asking, objections they may have, burdens which they bear, doubts and perplexities they have to face. It is a good plan to ask ourselves what we have to say to such and such an one, as the case comes to our notice. Nothing will challenge our minds more than to keep an open ear to the cry of spiritual need that is always breaking out, though it be unconsciously, from the defects and failures and sins of people around us. For all this, of course, we will need to be steeped in Scripture. It is both a means of keener insight into human need and a perfect answer to that need at whatever level we come upon it ; while, withal, it reaches depths we can neither see nor feel, searching the most hidden thoughts and intents of the heart. The open Bible, in every sense of the word, is the door that swings wide both to human need and God's grace: the twofold revelation which it holds is to every true preacher a perpetual and dazzling discovery.

Instinct will help us in our choice. If we are keen on our task, and thinking of our people, we will not naturally keep them on the same kind of diet. We will go in for contrasts. There is a danger of getting into ruts in our choice of subjects—a danger largely due to giving too little time to thought and study. We have a rushed week, and

we take the line of least resistance, which is
a text that makes an immediate appeal to
our circle of ideas. That is the danger of
reading for texts. We naturally choose that
which is capable of easy or popular exposi-
tion. The way to safeguard ourselves is to
read, not for preaching, but for life and for
truth. The preacher to whom the Bible is
a land of adventure for his own mind and
soul will have no difficulty about texts.

But one or two things are worth attention in choosing a subject. For one thing,
we should go in for the big texts. There was
a time when the ideal of many a preacher
seemed to be to search the Bible for some
little phrase or curious turn of a sentence,
that might become a peg for a neat discourse, well spiced with smart little epigrams.
That day is over. Serious people have no
time for sermons of that type. The others
will not be reached by it. Let us get back
to the big penetrating things about God, and
life, and the troubles of the heart, which it is
the business of the Bible to keep alive for us.
A text is not worth preaching on, that only
taxes our ingenuity. Take up a book of

sermons of Dale, or Beecher, or Phillips
Brooks, or Lecky of Ibrox—in fact, of any
man of more than a quarter of a century ago
whose name as a preacher still lives to-day
—and you will not find a trifling text in the
whole book. It is the subjects that engage
most deeply our own mind and spirit in
preparation for the pulpit, that find the most
ready audience when we come to preach—
provided we are really ready to preach on
them. Further, let us realize that the Bible
contains a body of teaching on the great
questions of life and destiny, and strive to
bring the full circle of its message to the
light. We need not intimate a series, let us
say, on the teaching of Jesus or the message
of Paul, but we should take care that the
congregation is made familiar with the truth
these represent. It is an excellent plan to
make a series of sermons out of a story like
the Prodigal Son, or a psalm like the Twenty-
third, or the various stages in the conversation of Jesus with the woman of Samaria, or
the different ways in which Jesus elicited
the practical response of faith in the people
He was about to heal or to bring into the

9

morning and evening. Most people are in
the habit of choosing for the morning something more solid, demanding a deeper level
of Christian experience; and for the evening,
something with a more popular appeal in the
best sense of the word, bearing in mind that
those who are on the fringe of religion, so
to speak, generally choose the evening for
their church attendance, and also the fact
that we shall probably have a larger number
of young people in the evening. Circumstances, of course, differ. The danger is of
falling into a habit, and forgetting—if our
plan is what I have outlined—that the people
who come in the morning may need the
" milk " as well as the "meat." Some of
them, it may be, may need, even more than
others, the elements of the gospel and the
note of the evangel, for the very reason that
their once-a-day attendance in the morning
may be the sign of a more or less formal
attachment. On the other hand, there will
be people who can only come in the evening,
but whose experience will demand the best
we can give them. I often take some of the
biggest subjects in the evening, though it

demands a bigger tax on my own mind to make the meaning intelligible, and keep the interest from flagging. As a general rule, of course, it is at the evening service that one would deal with subjects which are suited to beginners, to those who are feeling their way, to those whom we want to win for the first time. But it must never be forgotten that the audiences, even if we get two good congregations, will be largely different, and we must not fail to provide accordingly for definite and systematic teaching from the pulpit for both. As for the practice of choosing and advertising catchy titles, it would be surprising to learn that they ever achieved anything, except to cheapen the pulpit. It is certain that some of the preachers who use this method and hold the people, do not keep their audience by such expedients, though they may imagine they do : there is something in the man himself or his message which gets hold. It is a dangerous principle to think that we must stoop to win the ear of the people. The danger is that having stooped we may remain at the low level. Besides, people who go a verdict or a decision or a conviction ; but it will never be a verdict in the abstract, or a conviction in general, or a decision in a vacuum. It will be a verdict or a decision or a conviction, suggesting or demanding a definite act, or a definite attitude, in daily life. You will often have the experience of writing a sermon half through, and then finding yourself come to a full stop. Your mind is held up. The fount is dry. You may even begin to lose interest. Ten chances to one the real reason is that the truth has never gripped you with any definite intention. You have not been thinking with your people in your mind. You have no real and visible objective. The moment you pull yourself up and ask, What is the thing to achieve ? or, What am I driving at ? —and get that clear—the thing begins to kindle in your mind. Let me commend to you the simple questions which a great surgeon says he asks himself before an operation. What is it I want to do ? Is this the best means of doing it ? And is it worth doing ? This last question, of course, may sometimes bring the shock of realizing that the thing you have in mind is, after all, not worth saying, or you have said it a fortnight ago, in which case you will have to find another subject. But that question should come early enough in our choice of a subject to give us time to find another. Here, however, I would warn you against the danger of too readily laying aside a subject which has been selected, and with which headway has been made. One would almost say it should never be done. The very effort to conquer the difficulty will be an excellent discipline. And what is even more important — through that effort we may reach a penetration of thought and a suppleness of expression which will in the end surprise us and make the difficulty a real place of discovery.

In the second place, having found our main idea—the principle that lies behind—the next thing is to unfold it. There is no cut-and-dried rule for divisions, or for finding material to divide or expand. The most dangerous thing to do is to read, for the immediate purposes of preaching, sermons which others have written on the same text. I am not we mean the sermon to achieve. There are sermons which should proceed by a series of logical steps to a conclusion. There are some that should proceed by stating a principle and making deductions of a practical kind, in order. There are sermons where the best plan is to state your main principle or central truth, be it some aspect of God's love or care, or some exhortation to practical duty, then think of three or four conditions of need among your people, or three or four spheres of life in which the duty should be operative, and proceed to apply it to these. For my own part I believe in divisions. It is a great help to our own minds for one thing, and I am sure it is a help to the people. It is better, however, not to announce them beforehand. The element of surprise should not be neglected. If you specially want them to remember your points, you can recapitulate at the end, but recapitulation needs careful handling.

Having got your aim defined and your main line laid down, you can then proceed to get the sermon into shape for preaching.

III

I have said nothing up to this point as to the mode of preaching, whether by reading a manuscript or by more or less free and direct speech from notes.   No man can be dogmatic to another on this point, though he may advise.   There are many things to be said on both sides.   Reading from a manuscript has the advantage of delivering us from a certain nervousness ; it retains the possibility of a good style ; it gives balance ; it may secure against verbosity ; it gets down the thing you mean to say in the form in which you feel it is best said ; and to some extent, so far as language can do it, it captures and fixes the glow of the creative moment. Though it must be observed that there are read sermons which do no one of these things.   On the other hand, the danger of a read sermon is that it may be out of touch with the audience.   You can read a thing which you cannot naturally speak, and in a way you would never naturally say it to a group of people face to face. The only successful way to use a read sermon is to speak from it, regarding it as verbatim notes.

On the other hand, a sermon which is spoken more or less freely, or with only a few notes to guide the speaker, has numerous disadvantages. It opens the way to repetition and verbosity, and tempts to laziness and to a false dependence on the mood of the moment—sometimes it results in a large admixture of "hot air," instead of truth. Yet it has also many advantages. We get direct touch with the audience. We can use our material more pliably. With it, one is not in the danger of preparing a sermon as if it were to be preached in a vacuum. There is not the remotest doubt that the people prefer it, and that for the best of reasons, because it is more real and escapes the aloofness that often characterizes a read sermon, even when the preacher is throwing pointed shafts. I have noticed, again and again, where a man was half the time talking and half the time reading, that the interest faded as soon as his head got down to the manuscript, because for those moments his own attention was deflected. It is certain the audience would prefer to listen to a good sermon spoken, even with grammatical slips and an occasional sentence that never came to earth, rather than to the most carefully prepared address delivered from a manuscript. That may be a wrong preference, but if it be so, it is one of these melancholy weaknesses to which you will have to accommodate yourself. I think if I were to look back on my experience, I should have to admit that the best sermons I have listened to were those that were read from a manuscript. But I do not think that is a fair test, for the preferences of a student of theology, with all respect, are no guide to the tastes of the average man. There is this also to be taken into account. The times are changing, and there is a new demand for reality which I cannot but feel the method of direct speech helps to supply.

Whether we read fully or not, we have to keep in mind that a sermon is not meant to be a complete and more or less satisfactory production in itself—like, for instance, an essay or a book. People can read such at their leisure, absorb its flavour, study its niceties, and follow its reasoning. A sermon is the communication, through a person, of a message to persons who are there to listen for that moment and no longer. Keeping in mind that you have the moment—no more— and that it is the contact of mind with mind that is the business of that moment, you can choose your method.

But whether it be read or spoken with more or less freedom, there are some other things to be kept in mind about the sermon preparation, after you have got the aim and the main lines.

1. In the first place, the sermon should always be written. I am perfectly clear and unrepentantly dogmatic about this. Writing gives clearness. It enables us to solve those most difficult problems in sermon preparation—the transitions from one point to another. The danger of not writing is that you may think you can trust to the moment to get across the chasm. It looks only a step, and you just let it go at that, and then you find, when you come to delivery, that you need a bridge which you have not got. You cannot cross naturally and simply and

inevitably, and you lose your audience in a flying leap which they cannot follow because they have not the mental agility to trace the connection in your mind. Study the transitions. Be careful of your logic. Writing fully, or more or less fully, will greatly help you to do this : that is one advantage of it.

Another advantage is found in style and language. You will save yourself repetition. You will keep a good style. You will get balance and proportion, and not find, as you may do otherwise, that you have taken so long in your introduction that you have little left for the main substance. And it will really guard you against all kinds of mental slackness. One of the besetting sins of the ministry is indolence, including intellectual indolence.

2. In the second place, a sermon should be written in a speaking style, whether it is going to be read or not. This means short sentences, and sentences which are not involved with metaphor or dependent clauses. A great many ministers would improve their style and get home more directly, if after writing their sermons they would go over

10

them and strike out nearly all the conjunctions and relative pronouns. This sounds exaggerated. So it is, yet it is on the right lines; verbosity must go, if our style is to be good. A good many delightful phrases and attractive asides must be sacrificed. We have got to get to the end of the street in half an hour or thereabouts, and to take with us many people whose minds do not move quickly, so we have not time for many of the interesting sights upon the way. It is a fact that some preachers read their sermons, not because they cannot speak directly, but because they cannot deliver without reading what their sermons ordinarily contain. That is why a read sermon often misses the mark, and why, whether we read it or not, the sermon as written should be such that it would be possible to speak it. If our reason for reading is that it is too involved, too crowded, too delicate in its suggestions for free delivery, we had better take it to pieces and scrap a good deal of it.

Our language, then, must be simple and clear. There are words that sound most satisfying which mean little or nothing to the mind. Never use a latinized word if you can get a homely Saxon equivalent ; or a word of two syllables, if one will do. Mr. Asquith, introducing a book on the legacy of Rome, quotes Cardinal Newman with approval : " Latin is comparatively weak, scanty, and unmusical, and requires considerable skill and management to render it expressive and graceful." This is also true of latinized English. It may produce sententious oratory. It does not make for clear terse speech. The words that are in the heart and mouth of the ordinary man about real things are all short and simple. You may not think this is important ; yet it may make all the difference between success and failure of the message. As you cultivate a good simple style—one which conveys most exactly and clearly your meaning, the mark of a good style—you will find that in speaking freely it will become a native instrument. Simple words, however, do not necessarily mean simple or poor ideas, nor high-sounding phrases a profound intelligence. The exact opposite is often the case. Our business calls upon us to bring the most profound and moving ideas home to the minds of the simplest, to break through the walls of ignorance with a big message, to enter lowly doors with the whole counsel of God. It challenges all our resources of thought and imagination to take this big message through these lowly doors. It takes all our ingenuity of mind and heart. Many men are limited to-day in their capacity to take in spiritual truth, for reasons into which I need not enter. But if we cannot bring the message of God to bear on these people, whatever the level of intelligence, whatever the outlook, we have no message for our time. It can be done if we will set ourselves to it, and, from the point of view of reality in style, be mercilessly critical of our own work. I cull at random a few sentences which stress these conclusions. They are taken from a sermon by Henry Ward Beecher on the Church's Duty to the Slaves, in which he urges that the Church should be competent to supply the needs of the poorest and lowliest, alike with the most cultured and intelligent. " A man that is to the last degree cultured in thought and in

language may be acceptable to all men, so
that he present the universal letter of introduction—the feeling that brings heart to
heart, high and low. But often pulpits are
made partial by a way of treating subjects
that is partial and excluding. . . . Let a
man discuss the love of Christ not as a living,
flaming fact made clear to the comprehension
of every child, but as an abstract thing, and
he will remove it beyond the range in which
the common mind walks. As far as the
benefit of the average classes in society is
concerned, you might just as well preach in
Greek, as in abstract language. . . . The use
of latinized words and periphrases, in what
is called elegant speaking and fine writing,
is a common vice. There is a great tendency
on the part of writers and speakers to avoid
domestic words and colloquialisms, as they
are called. . . . What does home mean ?
When you speak that word it is as if you
struck a beehive and a thousand bees begin
to buzz and hum music in your mind. Father
and mother are words that children learn on
the hearth and in the nursery. . . . The
man that knows how, like old Bunyan, and

like Baxter, to take the Saxon colloquial terms of the household, of the kitchen, of the parlour, of the nursery, of the field, where men live, and employ them in his preaching, is a powerful and eloquent preacher. These old brawny, large-meaning words, heavily laden with precious associations, are words of might. But how many of our preachers, for the sake of being literary, for the sake of being polished, step aside from the great highway of power in language, into the little lanes of exclusiveness, where there is no power!"

IV

Let me say a word or two now regarding the various parts of the sermon. Let us think, to begin with, of the introduction. That will probably be the last part of the sermon you will prepare before writing it. Some people work for a striking introduction that they may win the ear of the audience at the beginning. It is possible to be too striking in one's introduction, so that two or three things may happen. The preacher may not be able to keep up the vivid interest of his beginning. He may draft off so much nervous attention on the part of the audience that they have nothing left to accompany him to the end, for it must be remembered that an audience has only a certain capacity in this direction, and can become nervously exhausted by something too hectic or thrilling at the start. Or, again, the preacher may make a false start and get the attention of the people by something which has really nothing to do with his line of thought ; in which case, when he has finished his introduction, he has by a violent transition to begin over again. His introduction in such a case is really a waste of time. Or, again, the introduction may be so obvious in its design of securing interest that it misses fire. The best way to begin is simply and naturally, remembering that the whole value of the opening sentences is to get on easy and natural terms with the people. The first thing we have to do is to bring our relation with the people in the matter of speaking and listening, to a basis of reality, so as to make them forget that *we* are preaching and that *they* are listening. It is best then to begin with something quite simple and easy, something that does not demand a great effort of mind. Relate the circumstances of the incident, or describe the context of the passage, or give a picture of the background; get the people, in short, into the feeling of the situation if it be an incident, or into the attitude of need or curiosity which first elicited the truth. The introduction will depend on our subject. It will also depend on our aim. It spoils a good sermon both to flounder about unable to rise from the ground, and to hover and circle uncertainly in the air because you have not made up your mind where you are to come down. But of that more anon.

With regard to the body of the sermon, little suggestion can in particular be made, except this, that a weak point or argument, or one comparatively unimportant in the movement, should come before a strong one, and our strongest point should come last. The stronger ones should be stated in stronger terms. If we are stating objections for the purpose of disposing of them, we must make sure that we do not state them so strongly

that our answers strike the audience as weak.
This is not to suggest any kind of juggling with
truth ; it is just dealing with a very common
fault. There are people who are tempted in
justice to an opponent to make an over-
generous statement of his case, and one which
they are not able to refute. If you cannot
put the truth more strongly and cogently
than the opposition to it, you are not ready
to preach on it. There is always the danger
that some in our audience may be caught
by something we say, and held so vividly
by it, that they miss the qualification which
follows. This is, of course, one of the difficulties about all preaching of the argumentative type.

It is useful to proceed occasionally by
question and answer, and not by a series
of bald statements. We must awaken the
people, challenge them to think, kindle their
minds to curiosity and search. Many of the
most impressive statements are made in the
form of the rhetorical question, though I use
that word " rhetorical " merely as a definition, for rhetoric is the born foe of reality
in preaching.

The use of fitting illustration will naturally engage our attention. Illustrations serve a double purpose. They illuminate—and they do so even more than we are aware—for life is always a medium for God's revelation. They give a rest both to the mind of preacher and hearer. They make a new jumping-off ground from which you can proceed with fresh power, while they arrest the flagging attention. Remember, that the average hearer is always looking to you to state your truth in terms of life, and illustration is one way of doing this. If we are trying to state a truth to a single hearer in conversation, it is highly probable that his mind is applying it and illustrating it for himself as we speak, if indeed he does not pull us up to ask us for a practical example. Illustrations should, of course, be fitting and to the point. Never put in an illustration for ornament. It is sure to be false. An illustration may be a picture flashed out in a phrase, or it may be a picture described at length, a story from history, an incident from literature. All great literature is great because it is a mirror of life, and a sound knowledge of literature is for this, among many reasons, essential to a preacher. It gives insight into aspects of life we cannot know at first hand. It does not much matter what illustrations a man uses provided they illustrate, and introduce no jarring note. The mood of one sermon will permit, as illustrations, stories of simple pathos, of tragedy, of experiences of our own, while the same kind of stories might be utterly out of place in sermons of another mood. We should never be afraid, however, to be simple and homely in our illustrations. In some respects the simpler these are, the better, always provided they help to make truth real. We will be quite safe, from the point of view of simplicity of style (though not, of course, of subject), in taking our audience on the level of children of thirteen or fourteen. The best illustrations, like the best quotations, are from the stories of Scripture, though it can never be taken for granted that they are known to the hearer, and they should be told as freshly and vividly as possible. There is drama there, and romance and poetry of the first order—all tested as the medium of spiritual truth by

a racial experience which is centuries old.
It has the additional advantage that it will
be new to at least some people, and will help
to increase their knowledge of Scripture, of
which the ignorance is colossal. I remember
reading not long ago, in a speech of one of
France's most prominent men, the remark :
" As the great English writer, Hall Caine,
has said, ' O death, where is thy sting ? ' "
You will not be preaching to a distinguished
Frenchman every day, but there is evidence
enough that this kind of ignorance is not
confined to the other side of the Channel.
Never forget this : in illustration, as in
everything else, the governing factor is that
our business is to get our message home,
not to write a beautiful or artistic sermon.
Everything must be subordinated to that.
An illustration which is not a medium, is
an intrusion, or a blind alley.

And now for the sermon's conclusion.
Do not study too much to end effectively.
The sermon ought to end when it is done,
when the message has got home. Stop when
you have finished. Stop with something
which will clinch your argument or point

your application. Do not be afraid, upon occasion, of the definite appeal, provided it be natural. If it be real, it will be effective. Never mind what people think, so long as you get there. But one thing should be said : we will probably find the need, again and again, of bringing our audience back to the central facts of the gospel. For it is a gospel we are preaching, even if we are outlining a duty or exhorting to some new attitude, and nothing we say to that end will be possible of achievement save in the atmosphere of the Christian resources. It is only in the presence of Christ, so to speak, that you can, for instance, bid your hearers love their enemies, or face some bitter road with patience, or take up some lonely burden with hope. Without the atmosphere of Christian love which penetrates and interpenetrates the Gospels, the Sermon on the Mount is so much dream-stuff, the starkest folly. It is only in the air of a spiritual world in which God is Father, that the way of Christ has power as well as music in it. If we do not also reveal the Christian life as a fellowship, the Christian ideal will do nothing for people but awake what Watson calls " the torment of the difference " ; and our business is to leave men with as deep a sense of the dynamic of duty or service, as of its stern compulsions. Consequently, all roads of argument or appeal will lead straight back to Christ, as Spurgeon boasted his sermons did. We will leave our people there to work it out with Him, more conscious of the strength than of the strain. " Courage and faith," says Stevenson somewhere, " is a good note to end on " ; but the highest note is that on which John Wesley ended his life : " The best of all is, God is with us." Wherever we lead our people in thought or daring or adventure, God's grace must dominate all.

V

Now let me speak just a word about delivery. If we are going to read our written sermon we must have it so prepared, so familiar to our mind, that it is supple. A sermon which goes into the pulpit with the ink barely dry is doomed to failure. We will not be in it, and if we are not in it, the power is gone. For preaching is truth mediated through personality, our eager, kindled, and invigorated mind. The best preachers from read sermons never give one a feeling they are reading.

As to the method of more or less free delivery, the best way is to read the sermon over carefully, thinking it out quietly the while, and to get into our mind several things—the illustrations, which will be an invaluable aid to memory and directness, the statement of our main truths in the form in which we want to convey them, the outline of our argument, and the conclusions on which we mean to end our chief points. We can be sure then that we will always be able to get home, even though we lose our way now and then on the road. To memorize a sermon and read it off the back of one's mind is like reading from a manuscript, so far as the distraction of our grip on the people is concerned. If we cannot do anything else than this we had far better read.

In delivery, use the conversational tone. We need elocution to deliver us from the unnatural voice and the false tone, and to give us voice production which will enable us to talk without strain or discomfort. Good natural voice production will go a long way to give the sense of reality. How much of the unreality of religion and the unreality of preaching itself, even in the material of a sermon, is due to the preaching voice, only the recording angel can compute. For there are things a man will say with an unnatural voice he would never dare to say in a conversational tone. It would sound too ridiculous. Reality in voice is a most powerful help to reality in impression and in the message itself. Why is it that when some men read the newspapers aloud they read simply, whilst whenever they begin to read the Scriptures they are like a man walking on stilts? I remember listening to a minister giving a political address. He was in real earnest, and it was simple, natural, gripping stuff ; but in the middle of it he had occasion to quote Scripture. At once he changed his note, and the people yawned till he was done. You cannot say, " God is love," in any kind of unnatural tone which will make it more impressive than it is.

How much the actual structure of the pulpit is to blame I do not know. I remember an Anglican clergyman whose service I attended beginning his service by coming out from the chancel to a little raised platform and talking to the people about prayer, in preparation for the service. It was a first-rate address, delivered naturally and simply, and the people were held. Then he went through the rest of the service, ending with a sermon from the pulpit. But the introductory address seemed the only thing that was real. The rest was like watching a man walking and talking in a dream. I sometimes think that most of our pulpits are too high. We have literally to talk down, and we get into the way of doing it metaphorically.

Of course a great deal of unnaturalness is due to self-consciousness, with which I want to deal later on. We start thinking of ourselves and so get on to a wrong note, and then do not know how to get off it. The audience feels it. They cough. They are restless. The sermon may be good enough. What is wrong? Ten chances to one it is the suggestion of strain, of unreality, in our

II

tone. We must somehow get on to natural terms with our audience, and a calm, quiet, natural voice will do it as nothing else will. Sometimes an interruption is a godsend. It may be the best thing that could happen, if we can take it so, and overcome it. It may knock us off the stilts, and bring us and the audience to the point where we have to talk realities in a real way.

In conclusion, let us remember we are not priests ; we are not even officials. We must even forget that we are ministers. Spiritual truth can only be mediated through relations that are simple and human. We can only help our fellows in the measure in which we can make them feel that we are one with them. The truth of the Incarnation has its point of glory and of power just there.

LECTURE V

THE PREACHER HIMSELF

IF any apology be needed for devoting a whole section to the preacher himself, it can be found in the definition of preaching as spiritual truth mediated through personality. Only through the right kind of personality can there be effective preaching. As Phillips Brooks puts it : " The preparation of a preacher is the making of a man." What makes a good preacher is what makes a good man. It may seem a daring thing to say, but the faults of much preaching are not primarily faults of style or manner or method, but faults of character. You do not get to the root of the faults till you get down to character itself. Milton has these striking words about the making of a poet which are also applicable to the making of a preacher : " He who would not be frustrate in his hope to write well in laudable things, ought himself to be a true poem ; that is, a composition and pattern of which has been possessing us for a while find its expression Godward if it be high, or its answer in God if it be low. We are depressed ; perhaps we do not know why. Then let us just face it, and search out for ourselves the consolations we need—the truths which in this sombre hour of the spirit when all kinds of drifting shadows are about, will bring the inextinguishable light. Thinking it out for ourselves, if we are real enough not to be put off with shelters and evasions, we shall discover the truth for others. Only what we ourselves are living by, can be really food for our people.

I

But to go deeper : the faults of much preaching—the big faults—are ultimately the faults of an outlook from which we are seeking to deliver our people. I have tried already to show what are the main defects in the outlook of people to-day.

There is fear, for instance ; and fear is one of the defects of the preaching temper. We may be tempted to be afraid of our audience, of some one in our audience. We may have an overweening concern for the sceptical or materialistic outlook of some individual, with the result that our preaching is strained to meet it, and so loses balance. We may, for instance, develop arguments that aim at meeting one special case, when what is wanted is a calm and confident faith in our message to meet every case. This universal message is, if only we knew it, just that for which people who appear to have a special need, are waiting. There is no greater mistake, by the way, than to try to rise to the intellectual level of some one person in our audience whom we are seeking to win. The best type of sermon is that which can be received by the woman from her kitchen and the scholar from his study. You will have them both in your audience, and you will have to find a medium that suits them both. Fear may arise from many causes. It may come from a sense of social or intellectual inferiority, or from the pride that hates to fail, and that cannot brook contempt or unpopularity or personal conflict. It is a curious fact in this connection, that the things we imagine will hurt people are not generally the things that actually do so. And the people we imagine may be hurt are often the last people to be so affected.

very truth may be the iron bars of ignorance
or real perplexity.   What seems a very little
difficulty may be the index of a trouble that
demands a radical change in the whole outlook.   This superior temper is often evident
in relation to wrong ideas of the older type.
We have to learn to be very patient with
those who differ from us and very humble in
our efforts to help them to see ; always, in
certain cases, " thinking it possible that we
may be mistaken," as Fox bade Cromwell do,
and never carrying the air of one who looks
wiser than any man is fit to be.   Let us not
forget that the real test of enlightenment is
whether it develops in us a more Christian
temper and helps us to do better service.
No advance in theoretical truth that does not
mean a personal advance for us in sympathy
with others and the power to understand
them is really a religious advance.   If the
truth we profess to have seen does not make
us better men than did the wrong outlook from
which we profess to have escaped, we may well
ask ourselves if we have really seen the truth
with that insight which means nearness to
Christ.   Paul's distinction is valid still : " Mere
knowledge puffeth up, but love buildeth up."

Yet again : may there not be religious unreality in our preaching because there is unreality in our lives ? Forgive me if here I suggest to you one peril of the ministry. It is to make the preaching of the gospel a substitute for walking in the way ourselves. Dr. L. P. Jacks says that " one of the most strongly marked features in the orator's moral psychology is a tendency to get confused between what he really believes himself and what he only wants other people to believe." This he applies particularly to political oratory, but we may well turn the searchlight on the preacher. Is it not just as true of us sometimes that " when principles we have advocated must be put into action we may make the discovery that in spite of our vehement desire that other people should believe in them, we have never believed in them ourselves " ? We speak of the love of Christ, and paint Him in colours which glow with the emotion of our hearts, but there may be nothing more. Our visions of love and righteousness and social duty may become a phantasy in which we live, making of it a substitute for a real experience and a patient service. Dante in the *Paradiso* to depend upon it. We shall be constantly trying to help our people to do their Christian work for " the joy of the working." We will need to take the same counsel to ourselves.

Another form of self is what we call self-consciousness. Some are more troubled by this than others. It is the frequent cause of the nervous breakdown. The symptoms are various. We may get stage-fright or something like it, and find it a struggle to face an audience. We may have a lapse of memory and become haunted by the fear of breaking down. Self-consciousness may come, of course, from causes that are purely physical. No man has any right to neglect his health : his whole spiritual outlook will suffer, and what he takes for some sickness of the soul or some prophetic vision of a world going to destruction, may only be due to a disordered digestion. But more often than not the cause of self-consciousness lies deeper. It may be a sense of inferiority springing from the struggle in youth against long odds, and demanding for compensation and for confidence some reward of ambition to set against a world that once ignored or despised us. The man wants to succeed. He is ambitious. He becomes afraid of failure. He is morbidly sensitive to any want of recognition. His joy in preaching is a form of self-glorification. His fine passages are all a source of vanity. It is a poor picture I am drawing, but it is a very true one, and reveals a peril familiar to many preachers. The real trouble, where a man is a victim to it, is that he is not really out for the Kingdom of God ; success or failure are all turned inward. It is fatally easy to seek ourselves when we think we are seeking the souls of men. And many a man is aware of it. He may indeed apply to himself a veritable scourge, and make all kinds of efforts to escape from the prison-house of self. And often in vain. For self-consciousness is a perfect prison-house, and a wise man will take sharp measures with it at the very beginning of its tyranny. In all its subtle forms it is the ruin of power and peace. The liberation of our personality in all sorts of ways comes through emancipation from self, and how to effect this escape is worth learning at the beginning of our ministry. One way is to become absorbed in the truth we have to speak, and in the needs of the people to whom we have to speak it.   I have known preachers find complete deliverance from this form of nervousness just by looking at the people and thinking quietly of their needs and of the task of helping them.   A nervous person trying to cross a stream by a narrow plank must look, not at the stream, but at the opposite bank which he wants to reach. To see the world as it is, and to realize afresh our own call from God to help it, will soon deliver us from self-consciousness.   If our self-consciousness should arise from a sense of our own defects and unfitness, a thing which cripples more men than we are aware of, the way to escape from that, is to realize that such self-humiliation is often a disguised form of pride :   to resolve just to accept our limitations and stop thinking about them ; doing the very best we can and leaving the quality of our work to be judged by our conscience solely on the ground of faithfulness. One of the most fatal diseases that can overtake a minister, apart from the itch for popularity, is to become sensitive about what others —especially other ministers—may think of his preaching.   Everything that takes a sermon out of its proper environment, which is the

mood in which it is written and the audience
it is meant for, and makes us judge it like a
picture or a bit of artistic furniture, is bad
for preaching. It is a wrong standard to use
in our preparation, and it is equally the wrong
standard for criticism whether of our own
work or that of others. We ought to help
one another—even to criticize one another—
but only in sincerity and with the true aim of
preaching in view, which is to help people to
see God—never to produce something that is
fine. There is a criticism of preaching which
is simply fuel to those hidden fires of vanity
or of bitterness that lay waste the power of
many a man. We have got to get into the
position of St. Paul: " For me it is a very
small matter that I should be judged of you
or of man's judgment. Yea, I judge not
mine own self. But He that judgeth me is
the Lord." And the things that count so
much with the undiscerning crowd on the
one hand, and with the superfine critic on
the other, count very little with Him.

Let me touch on one point more in this
connection. If we have ability, brains, a gift
of expression, some power of attraction, let us
thank God for them. That is the real way to

12

perfect self-forgetfulness is perfect self-fulfil-
ment. The release of personality in preaching
is very largely the deliverance from self-
consciousness.

Believe me, these are things of which I
speak with trembling. Yet I feel most
deeply that they go to the heart of the whole
matter. The preacher who is not a good
man will not be a good preacher. He may
be popular ; he will have no real power.
The ministry is the last calling in which
selfish ambition can make for success, for
that ambition is the surest way to failure.
It cuts the nerve of spiritual power. To be
out for a career, in the ordinary sense of the
word, is to lose touch with the Kingdom of
God. " Thank God that He hath counted
me worthy, putting me into the ministry."
The more we approximate to that position,
the more will the joy of the Lord, which is the
joy of creating new things and redeeming
broken things, become our strength.

III

Let me speak now of some of the qualities
which preaching needs for its highest effectiveness. The first of these is *sympathy*. We

must be one with our people. We must
know them, think with their thoughts, understand their outlook, put ourselves resolutely
in their place. You remember Ezekiel when
he went to speak to the exiles in Babylon.
" I went down by the river and I sat where
they sat." Was that a literal getting into
their place, or was it only a metaphor for
imaginative sympathy ? It must be both with
us, and both at the same time. Imaginative
sympathy is the quality we most need in
pastoral visitation. It is the one way in
which we shall be able to speak the word
our people need for the healing of some
wound or the quickening of some nerve.
Lord Acton says of George Eliot : " She had
the secret not only of reading the diverse
hearts of men but of creeping into their skins,
watching the world with their eyes, feeling the
latent background of conviction, discerning
theory and habit ; and having obtained this
experience, recovering her independence."
We must acquire this habit of sympathy if
we have not already got it, till it become
real and natural, and carefully cultivate it if
it be a native gift. May I repeat again the
suggestion that there are two kinds of

ministers ?—the one more interested in ideas than he is in people ; the other more interested in people than he is in ideas. This latter is the true minister. The last thing I would dream of is to cast any reflection upon the scholarly minister whose real home is in the study, and who finds contact with people disturbing. He is doing his special work. Yet, in general, I think the definition stands, searching though it is to those of us who feel the fascination of a big subject and the adventure of working it out. It is *people* who must be foremost in our minds, people we can help with the truth, people to whom it will be the message from God. We must get to thinking out truth for our people with them in view, searching for it as a man on the moor might search for a lost child for the joy of finding it, but most of all for the joy of taking it home and restoring it to the arms of its mother. Believe me, you will find a new glory in the truth when you have seen it kindling the light in some lack-lustre eye. Dr. Fraser tells in *African Idylls* how he put on his gramophone a record of the Hallelujah Chorus that a native might hear it. He describes the effect on this man, and then adds: "He went off, leaving me more solemnized by music than I had ever been before, for I had seen one to whom it had opened the gates of heaven and revealed the glories ineffable." An unselfish interest in truth is a vital necessity for a preacher. It is the basis of the preacher's passion. We will need sympathy if we are not to be accused of fumbling with men's troubles, treating symptoms without getting to the roots of the disease, " healing the hurt of the daughter of my people slightly," offering a comfort that is no consolation, making a false appeal. We will need sympathy, even if we are going rightly to condemn. No man has any right to judge his fellows whose tongue is sharpened by censoriousness or by self-righteousness, or who is moved by anything less than the pain of his own shamed and saddened spirit, feeling the wrong he judges as if he had in some sort been responsible for it, or shared the guilt of it. That place of moral kinship with the one who is guilty is the only safe place of judgment, and that is the place of sympathy. It is not enough to be sorry *for* a man; we must be sorry *with* him, and ashamed with him, before indignation becomes a weapon of love. And that takes sympathy.

Most of all it is by sympathy that we are helped to recover the evangelical passion when we have lost it, or when it has begun to flag. You will have a unique experience if there do not come days when you ask yourself in some low mood : " Why should I preach, after all ? Why go on preaching ? After all, these people are living fairly good and harmless lives, and these others outside the churches seem to need very little that one can say to them, and seem to get on very well without religion. Why need we trouble ? " Moods like that come to us all. I am stating it bluntly because it is better to face facts. We banish them, of course, and they go after a longer or a shorter time. But perhaps in banishing them thus we have lost something, or taken for escape some lower ground on which we are content to stand, and become satisfied with preaching which is passionless and conventional. Now the real way to recover the evangelical passion, apart from the recovery of our own experience of the grace of God, is so to steep ourselves in the needs of others that the gospel message takes new fire in our own hearts. It is to get into the lives of people, into their circumstances, to feel their pitiful futility, their trivial satisfactions, their uneasiness and hunger of spirit, their mean ambitions, their pathetic struggles, their sorrows ; and every now and then, just because you are *en rapport* with people, you will get a sudden look into the abyss, where the ground opens at your very feet in some commonplace or apparently happy home. And with a thankful heart you will realize what it means to have a gospel, what it means to be " delivered from the power of darkness and translated into the Kingdom of God's dear Son, in whom we have redemption through His blood, even the forgiveness of sins."

I have said that this habit of sympathy is one that can be acquired, apart even from our own actual experience of the same kind of trouble as that which calls it forth. This may seem doubtful. But there are instances to prove it. A curious fact is that those who look on from without at some trouble which others are bearing, may often feel its pain through imagination even more than those who are within it, because they feel the pain without at the same time sharing in the compensations which suffering often brings. There is an incident in Stevenson's life which illustrates what I mean. One of his most bracing books was written at Bournemouth in the midst of paralysing weakness. A hæmorrhage prevented him from speaking, an attack of writer's cramp from writing, and his eyesight was also affected by some temporary malady ; but he dictated the book to his wife by means of the dummy alphabet ! One can hardly imagine any situation more devastating to a brave outlook on life. When the book was published a critic attacked its philosophy on the ground that the man who wrote it could have had little experience of the sterner side of life. Stevenson wrote him, describing the actual conditions under which the book was done, whereupon the critic replied that in that case he must have been writing it with his tongue in his cheek. Stevenson's answer to this was that a spectator of some trouble may often feel it more than one who is experiencing it, because he knows nothing of the interior consolations,

Experience, of course, is one of the ways in which God can soften our hearts to the pain of others, but it is not essential. If we arc willing to think ourselves into the situation of others, we can acquire the habit of sympathy. A case in point is that of Dale of Birmingham. His son describes it thus: " He was not selfish, but he was apt to be self-absorbed, engrossed by his own thoughts, and so abstracted as to be heedless of those whom he met, and of what was going on around him. His nature was not sympathetic. The faculty so freely bestowed on some, he had to cultivate sedulously and patiently, as one of the moral virtues. And as it not infrequently happens, the faculty thus acquired proved the stronger and richer for the effort and trouble it had cost in the winning."

In what I have said above I have suggested, without stating it in so many words, what sympathy is. But it is well before we leave the subject to ask what real sympathy is. For until we see what it is, we cannot make it really effective. What does it mean to have sympathy, for instance, with a person who has just discovered that

he has become a victim to cancer? Or
with one who is facing irretrievable ruin in
business? Or with another whose home is
stricken by sorrow after sorrow? Sympathy
is not merely feeling with another in his
suffering. We may feel and feel deeply,
entering with heart and imagination into his
situation, in a way that really makes us one
with him in his pain. We may express our
sympathy with him in words or in deeds
that are very tender and bring a real sense
of the consolation of friendship, which in
itself can be a veritable ministry of God.
He will find comfort in the sense that he is
not alone, which is the lesson that, as legend
tells us, Buddha taught the woman who had
lost her child and was grief stricken. He
sent her to seek a black mustard seed, which,
however, she must not take from a house
where any one had died. The comfort he
meant her to find was, of course, the knowledge that sorrow is the burden of all, and
so her grief might grow less by the sense
that it was shared. But that kind of
sympathy is not the deepest or truest. Our
depth and poignancy of feeling, for instance,
may only come from the secret sense that

we have no real remedy, and that in the like case we would be in hopeless despair. This seems very subtle, but any minister who looks into his own heart will realize how true it is. Effective sympathy goes deeper. It means not only feeling with sorrow, but also facing it with God ourselves and finding in Him the answer to the trouble; it goes forth then to the sufferer holding out a hand which has grasped the hand of God and so is strong to minister real comfort. We dare not go to another in pain or sorrow except in the strength of a faith that has touched rock-bottom and found it secure. That kind of sympathy is not less tender, but there is strength also in it, and the light of victory, and the confidence that, having overcome the world in this special instance of its power to wound, it carries with it the sure secret of the power to overcome.

This, of course, seems to have more particular reference to our pastoral work. But it holds also in our preaching. In point of fact, our power in the pulpit is only an extension of the same personal intimacy which gives us power in individual dealings. Unless we can bridge the distance between the pulpit

and the pew by this intimate sympathy, our
preaching will be of none effect.   It will be
but " sounding brass or a tinkling cymbal."

Another quality we shall need is *confidence
in our message*.   Think of Jesus for a moment
in this connection.   How He went about
saying, to this one and that one, great,
miraculous, unbelievable things, like " Thy
sins be forgiven thee " to a man whose past
was like a mountain wall ; and " Take up
thy bed and walk " to a lifelong cripple ;
and " Your Father knoweth that ye have
need " to people who were mere insignificant
things in a merciless world.   They just took
it for granted, and amazing things happened.
There must have been in Him, and in His
quiet utterance and manner, a confidence
that produced the conviction that the thing
He was saying was real—no dream, no
formula, no vague hope of better things.
And this confidence somehow communicated
itself to the people to whom He spoke, so
that they " believed in His belief."   Without doubt, the power of Jesus to break the
chain of moral impotence which bound many
people, was that He gave them power,
through His very faith in them, to believe

in themselves. Was not His message to
people, after all, just the possibility of goodness, of purity, of victory there and then ;
the sense that they were living in a spiritual
world, in which they had only to begin to
draw breath, without any magical rites or
purifications ? Of course this simple call to
people to begin to live a natural, spiritual
life was made in full view of the resources
which are in God to meet their need, at
work for them, and in Him able to make
all things possible. When He told a man
his sins were forgiven, the man accepted
the fact as Christ meant him to do ; and
when He bade the lame man walk, the
lame man did it without any more ado
than if He had asked him to eat his break-
fast. Christ expected this response, and the
man never had any doubt the thing would
happen. Have we this confidence and the
power of imparting it ? When we tell people
that if only they come to Christ their lives
will be changed, do we believe it ? Do we
believe that faith in God will enable a man
to face the impossible ? Do we believe in
the wonderful things which we claim for the
gospel ? I sometimes wonder if the im-

potence of the message does not often spring from a latent scepticism in the preacher's heart. We have to be on our guard against this. Nothing so quickly communicates itself to others as the subconscious mood of doubt or unbelief. Indeed, it is a question whether what we *are* in those dim regions of our spirit does not speak so loudly, awakening suggestions and raising questions in the minds of those to whom we speak, that they cannot hear what we say. The same, I would add, is true of public prayer, though this forms no part of our subject. There is a subtle scepticism which often slays reality. It is good sometimes to put to ourselves the questions : Do I really mean this ? Is this really true ? Do I expect these things to happen ? Would we be more rejoiced or more nonplussed if there should be an invasion some Sunday night into the vestry of one or another challenging us ? "Is what you have been saying to-night a fact ? How can I really secure the gift ? " There is little doubt but that the attitude of expectancy on our part communicates itself to the people. If you expect things to happen, you have produced the atmosphere in which things do happen, whether you hear of it before the Day of Judgment or not.

Again, the preacher must be *whole-hearted*. It is woefully possible to do our work with half our personality asleep or unemployed. The psychologists are telling us that few people ever work up to the level of their innate possibilities. We have to bring our whole mind to the preparation of a sermon for one thing. It is no good going on with the full extension of our notes till our whole capacity for thought and feeling has been brought to bear on it. The illuminating moment, when we reach, as it were, the crest of the hill and see the landscape of truth stretching out in various directions, only comes when our whole mind is in the subject. Nearly every man who deals with preaching condemns laziness as our besetting sin. How much this is due to lack of concentration, so that the immediate trifling things get first call and keep us busy on futilities, and how much to indolence, is a question. Indolence, however, is rooted in lack of vital interest. There is a certain amount of drudgery which must be got through, and for that there is nothing but to set our face

13

and go through with it. But where our
whole interest is engaged we do not think
of the toil, and do not require to whip ourselves to our task. We think nothing either
of time or effort when we are busy at our
hobby. Our wills follow the path of our
interest. Preaching may begin to lack
interest because from our very conscientious-
ness to do the work well, religion becomes
isolated as our special department, and not
the key to all our interests. Our work comes
to have the feel of an external duty, in which
our whole nature is not running freely and
harmoniously. That seems to me to be
nearest the truth.

However it comes about, if we are not in
our work—all we are and all the time—the
defect is fatal. The hours of study must
be rigidly guarded. Some people inveigh
against the slavery of turning out two
sermons a week. It seems to me that for
many preachers the necessity has been invaluable. I have never found that I produced a better sermon when I had, by some
chance, only one to prepare. Most of us
work better under pressure. "A man's work
may be his best life preserver," some one

has said.   It is eminently true of the preacher.
In the preparation of a sermon, let us be in
it whole-heartedly, with every scrap of
capacity, imagination, memory, ingenuity,
that we have.

This brings me to say that true preaching
demands *abandonment*.   It means giving
ourselves away.   Some of us are so afraid
of what a good elder of mine calls "spilling
over."   We consciously reserve ourselves.
That is all right at the beginning of a sermon.
But when the truth gets hold of us and we
want to express it, for any sake never mind
the proprieties.   We must think of our
message and of the people, and let everything else go.   We may often say a foolish
thing, and an exaggerated thing, in the heat
of the moment.   The people would far rather
have the heat than the precision of calculated
statement.   And the heat of a great truth is
often part of the true statement of it, though
emotional expression differs.   But do not be
afraid of giving yourself away.   How that
self-giving will shape itself is a matter of
temperament.   But aloofness has generally
something unnatural behind it.   It may be
that just the act of breaking free of all the

entanglements of nervousness, whatever they are, may be the best means of snapping the bondage of self-consciousness. I remember in the first year of my ministry how I was taken to task by one of the most gifted laymen the Presbyterian Church in Scotland has ever had, the late Dr. Taylor Innes. I had preached what I felt was rather a poor sermon. He happened to be in the congregation, and kindly asked me to come and see him next day, which I gladly did. " Now," he said genially, " I am going to talk to you, for I am rather an authority on preaching. I once lectured to the New College Theological Society at their opening meeting, with Principal Rainy in the chair, on ' Why are our New College students not good preachers ? ' " Then he went on: " You thought that was rather a poor sermon last night ? " " Yes," I said. " Yes," he went on, " you very successfully communicated that to the congregation. Well, you are going to ruin your ministry just there. If you have done your best with a sermon, whether you think it good or not, take it as a message and give it a chance. Put yourself into it with all its seeming defects. More promising preachers fail through this want of abandonment than for any other cause." I pass on this counsel for what it is worth. I think it is worth a good deal. Of course it is dangerous advice. To a fool, all the best advice is dangerous. The gospel itself is the most dangerous of doctrines—the gospel of forgiveness and the grace of God. There is always the danger that advice like that of Dr. Innes may make a fool imagine that bluster will take the place of brain, or that man will hear us—any more than God—for our much or our loud speaking. But the advice is sound. We must give ourselves away in our preaching, caring for nothing, so long as we get the truth home.

" O the gravity, the seriousness, the incessant diligence which these things require," wrote Richard Baxter. " I am ashamed that such astonishing matters do not wholly absorb my mind. I seldom come out of the pulpit but my conscience reproacheth me that I have been no more serious and fervent in such a case. It accuseth me, not so much for want of ornaments or elegancy, nor for letting fall an unhandsome word ; but it asketh me, How couldst thou speak of life

and death with such a heart ?   Truly this is
the peal which conscience doth ring in our
ears.   O Lord, do Thou that on our own
souls which Thou wouldst use us to do on
the souls of others."

This giving of ourselves is no easy thing.
It involves sacrifice.   Francis Thompson says
that " Every poem is a human sacrifice."
Joseph Parker said that " Preaching is the
sweating of blood."   Both mean the same
thing.   And what does the New Testament
say of Jesus, summing up His life and death
in one act.   He gave Himself.   It will mean
sacrifice for us.   Through the whole service
of the ministry, what we do for people in any
real and helpful way is just to give them
ourselves.   And only as that is done sacri-
ficially, in the unselfish spirit of Christ, will
the alabaster box be broken and the house
be filled with the odour of the ointment.

It all comes to this, does it not ?   We can
only help people, only bring them into touch
with redeeming love, in the measure in
which we mediate, through our preaching,
the Spirit of Christ.   You cannot account
for Christ's power with men by His message

alone. It was Himself giving it, Himself saying these words, and Himself creating the atmosphere by His Spirit in which great truths become believable, and the step of trust and faith is taken. In the same way, you cannot account for the success of the apostles, bringing men and women under the power of the gospel and casting out devils, except by the fact that their lives suggested Jesus. Stephen's preaching helped, no doubt, to stake a claim for Christ in Paul's mind, but it was Stephen's death suggesting Jesus and setting His Spirit free, that made the final conquest. " In the name of Jesus of Nazareth," said Peter to the lame man, " I say unto thee, Rise up and walk." The name could hardly be enough. There must have been something in the whole quality of Peter's personality that revealed Jesus. A preacher in his preaching must mediate Jesus, mind and soul together, or there is no possibility of a miracle. We must convey the sense of God's forgiveness, His friendship, His sympathy with outcast men, His challenge to people—not merely use words about it. And that means we must feel these things ourselves, and have the same attitude as He towards the people to whom we are speaking, or little of the sense of spiritual realities will filter through our words or shape our language into a channel for God's grace. It is just here that the prophet becomes the priest in any healthy sense, where the message is able to mould men, because it has first of all moulded us into a medium, where " mind and soul, according well, may make one music."

Let me recapitulate. Our task is to make real, God in Christ, so as to bring into fellowship with Him, people who are estranged from Him in wrong thinking, in wrong desires, in wrong attitudes to life, and in wrong relations to one another. " We are ambassadors for Christ," says Paul. " We therefore beseech men, in Christ's stead, to be reconciled to God." That must be the whole spirit of our preaching. " We are ambassadors ": we represent God in a world where He is misunderstood. " We beseech men ": that is our final weapon. " In Christ's stead ": that is our tremendous responsibility and our privilege alike—to reveal Jesus in all our ministry. Our only glory is to be like Him. " Wherefore he that hath this hope in him, purifieth himself, even as He is pure."